With heart-felt thanks for
the lift home last Friday!

Peter Leggett

18 : 6 : 90

THE SACRED QUEST

Other publications by D. M. A. Leggett

A FORGOTTEN TRUTH
(with Max Payne)

WAR GAMES THAT SUPERPOWERS PLAY
*(Booklet with C. M. Waterlow, now
in its third edition)*

Contributed to
HARVEST OF LIGHT
(ed. Neville Armstrong)

THE PSYCHOLOGY OF NUCLEAR CONFLICT
(ed. Ian Fenton)

THE
SACRED QUEST

BY EXPERIMENT AND EXPERIENCE –
THE NEXT STEP

D. M. A. LEGGETT

M.A. *(Cantab)*, D.Sc. *(Lond)*
D.Univ. *(Surrey)*, F.R.Ae.S.
F.I.M.A., F.K.C.

One time Fellow of Trinity College, Cambridge
Formerly Vice-Chancellor of Surrey University

PILGRIM BOOKS
TASBURGH NORWICH ENGLAND

British Library Cataloguing in Publication Data

Leggett, D. M. A.
The sacred quest: by experiment and
experience – the next step.
1. Life
I. Title
128'.5   BD431

ISBN 0–946259–19–4

Photoset by Waveney Typesetters, Norwich
and printed in Great Britain by the Oxford University Press

Contents

Foreword by Sir Kelvin Spencer   vii
Prologue   xi
Acknowledgements   xii
Personal Introduction   1

Part I – The Quest
1   Education – For What?   7
2   Clearing the Ground   14

Part II – Evidence
3   From Mysticism   31
4   From Poetry   42
5   From the Paranormal   51
    5.1   Out-of-Body Experiences   51
    5.2   Survival   62
    5.3   Reincarnation   70

Part III – What the Evidence Indicates
6   Some Propositions   93
7   The Purpose of Human Life I   98
8   The Purpose of Human Life II   113
9   The Purpose of Human Life III   133
10 The Potentialities of the Ordinary Man or Woman   144

Part IV – Application
11 Guidelines   159
12 Virtue and Vice – What it Means to be Good   175
13 Evil, Sin and Suffering   189
14 The Fruit of Experience   204
15 Implications for Education   212
    Epilogue   224
    Appendices I and II   225
    Bibliography   228
    Index   233

This book is dedicated to my family,
who have taught me so much

Foreword

Some three centuries ago what is now known as the scientific method of thinking emerged from a long struggle for freedom of thought. Now, in the last quarter of the twentieth century, this framework on which to organise thought has become so dominant that most of us do not realise that it is but one of many on which, down the centuries, communities have unconsciously organised their thoughts. In its own field scientific materialism has been conspicuously successful. To science we owe most of the material comforts of modern life: electric light, freedom – for some – from laborious drudgery, anaesthetics, and advances in medicine to which many owe relief from pain and illness. The list of benefits is long: benefits all relevant to our material welfare.

But these benefits have been at a cost. Mankind seems to have lost all sense of purpose. And too often the apparent benefits have turned out to bring in their train great evils: the atomic bomb, napalm, thalidomide, and the like.

The nineteenth century was an age of optimism. Science seemed to promise answers to all our troubles if only we pursued it with vigour and determination. This optimism has since dwindled.

Towards the end of his life H. G. Wells (1866–1946) wrote a small book, *Mankind at the End of its Tether*, which came strangely from one who had spent his life in popularising and praising science in all its many aspects. He wrote:

> Our world of self-delusion will perish amidst its evasions and fatuities. It is like a convoy lost in darkness on an unknown

rocky coast, with quarrelling pirates in the chart-room and savages climbing up the sides of the ship to plunder and do evil as the whim may take them . . . Mind near exhaustion still makes its final futile movement towards that 'way out or round or through the impasse' . . . There is no way out or round or through . . . There is no Pattern of Things to Come . . . Homo sapiens, as he has been pleased to call himself, is in his present form played out.

A few decades later Julian Huxley in *The Essays of a Humanist* wrote:

> Science has removed the obscuring veil of mystery from many phenomena . . . but it confronts us with a basic universal mystery – the mystery of existence in general, and of the existence of mind in particular.

More recently still Alister Hardy in *The Divine Flame* strikes a similar note:

> Could it be possible that modern humanistic man, excited by the success and neatness of the scientific method, and exalted by a sense of liberation from the intellectual absurdities of mediaeval thought, has been carried away into a new realm of intellectual folly quite different from but only a little less absurd than that which preceded it. Could he be making a gigantic mistake?

Dr Leggett's book to which I am privileged to write this Foreword challenges this line of pessimistic thought and gives a much more hopeful and inspiring message. His book is a bridge across the chasm which too often separates two ways of interpreting life – the scientific way and the religious way.

Many of us, less now than hitherto, were brought up in a formal dogmatic religious faith which, as we mixed with our contemporaries, we found few really believed. All too common a response was to assume that religion and the dogmas of a particular sect were one and the same thing; and a frequent response was to reject both. This has culminated in a materialistic outlook which is a denial of the whole basis on which our civilization was born and matured. This civilization, which is now showing ominous signs of disintegration, had a spiritual basis of which so many are now ignorant or which is now derided as a curious and outmoded way of thinking.

It has long seemed probable to me that we are living in one of the ages when evolution takes a jump forward. The geological record gives evidence of several such jumps; for instance, when aquatic life emerged onto the land and into the air, and when the forerunners of homo sapiens deserted the trees for the ground. The evolutionary jump we seem now to be taking is not one of the physical body. It is an evolution of mind, consciousness, awareness: a spiritual evolution. Science so far has ignored this. One of the quotations in Chapter 1 of Dr Leggett's book drives this home:

> There has simply been little interest on the part of science in the great spiritual questions of human life. Religious concerns have often been callously dismissed as illusory panaceas, power politics and pathology. But if science is supposed to serve the whole man, it is indeed a scandal that a huge proportion of our civilization's human and material resources has been absorbed by a *sub-culture which has systematically screened out the study of the transcendent and the ultimately human.* (My emphasis.)

The Sacred Quest will, I hope, help to widen the self-imposed boundary of contemporary thought which impedes the development of a wider awareness. For this expansion of awareness, is, I believe, the next step in evolution – a step we now have freedom to hasten or delay. Indeed, if our freedom is wrongly used and we continue our reckless ravaging of the earth's stored riches for purely material ends, we may render further development of life on this planet impossible.

Dr Leggett gives us some guideposts to help us on our way. Let us collaborate with life towards a goal which we can as yet but dimly imagine, but which to many is a 'lasting inspiration, sanctified by reason and by truth'. This book will, I hope, sound a chord which will find an echo in the hearts of many who feel as I do, that it speaks –

'A lasting inspiration, sanctified
By reason and by truth; what we have loved,
Others will love; and we may teach them how;
Instruct them how the mind of man becomes
A thousand times more beautiful than the earth
On which he dwells, above this Frame of things,
(Which, 'mid all revolutions in the hopes
And fears of men, doth still remain unchanged)
In beauty exalted, as it is itself
Of substance and of fabric more divine.'

(Wordsworth, *Prelude*, Book xiv)

Sir Kelvin Spencer, M.C., C.B.E., B.Sc.

Prologue

We are now reaping the fruit of nineteenth-century education. Throughout that period the Church preached to young people the merit of blind faith, while the universities inculcated an intellectual rationalism, with the result that today we plead in vain whether for faith or reason. Tired of this warfare of opinions, the modern man wishes to find out for himself how things are. And though this desire opens the door to the most dangerous possibilities, we cannot help seeing it as a courageous enterprise and giving it some measure of sympathy. It is no reckless adventure, but an effort inspired by deep spiritual distress to bring meaning once more into life on the basis of fresh and unprejudiced experience.[1]

C. G. Jung

References

1. *C. G. Jung: Psychological Reflections*, Jolande Jacobi, (Routledge & Kegan Paul, 1971), p. 284

Acknowledgements

In writing *The Sacred Quest* I have received much assistance from many people, and to all of them I welcome this opportunity of expressing my thanks and appreciation. I am especially indebted to Mrs Helen Greaves, Mr Max Payne, and Mrs Jean Sydney for reading and commenting on an early draft; to Mrs W. D. Woods for her comments and for typing the final manuscript; and to Sir Kelvin Spencer for a particularly lengthy and penetrating list of comments, and for his thought-provoking Foreword. Whatever merit the book may have is largely due to help thus received.

I am glad to record that many of the topics discussed in *The Sacred Quest* have been the subject of talks I gave at meetings of the Churches' Fellowship for Psychical and Spiritual Studies, the College of Psychic Studies, or the Centre for Spiritual and Psychological Studies. In addition I wish to thank the following persons and publishers for permission to quote from their books, journals, and papers: American Society for Psychical Research, Inc. for extracts from article by Ian Stevenson in the Society's *Journal*; Aquarian Press for extracts from *The Study and Practice of Astral Projection* by Robert Crookall; Blackie and Son for extract from *The Flame and the Light* by Hugh Fausset; the Churches' Fellowship for Psychical and Spiritual Studies for extract from *Testimony of Light* by Helen Greaves; the City Temple for extract from article by the then Minister, Rev. Leslie Weatherhead; James Clarke & Co. for extracts from *The Supreme Adventure* by Robert Crookall; Doubleday & Co. Inc. for extract from *Journeys out of the Body* by Robert A. Monroe; Edward Arnold for extracts from *The Human*

ACKNOWLEDGEMENTS

Situation by W. Macneile Dixon; Faber & Faber for extract from *The Psychic Sense* by P. D. Payne and L. J. Bendit; George Allen & Unwin for extract from *Conquest of Illusion* by J. J. van der Leeuw; Hodder & Stoughton for extracts from *Watcher on the Hills* by Raynor C. Johnson; Hutchinson Publishing Group for extracts from *The Problem of Rebirth* by Ralph Shirley, and from *The Occult Way* and *Sayings of the Ancient One* by P. G. Bowen; Jonathan Cape and the Estate of Robert Frost for 32 lines from 'Trial by Existence' by Robert Frost; Mrs Laura Huxley and Chatto & Windus for extract from *The Perennial Philosophy* by Aldous Huxley; Landscot for extract from article by Maurice Blake in *East Anglia Monthly*; Lucis Trust for extracts from *Unfinished Autobiography*, *Discipleship in the New Age* Vol. II, *Externalisation of the Hierarchy*, *Treatise on Cosmic Fire*, and *The Labours of Hercules* by Alice A. Bailey; Macdonald Futura Publishers for extract from *Frontiers of Revelation* by Frances Banks; Neville Spearman for extracts from *The Boy Who Saw True* collated by Cyril Scott, *A Man seen Afar* by Wellesley Tudor Pole and Rosamond Lehmann, *The Silent Road* by W. Tudor Pole, and *Many Mansions* by Gina Cerminera; Peace Through Unity for extract from *Let Life Live* by Gita Keiller; Psychic Press for extract from *Survival of Death* by Paul Beard; Routledge & Kegan Paul for extract from *Swan on a Black Sea* by Geraldine Cummins; Spiritual Frontiers Fellowship for extract from article by Rev. J. Schoneberg Setzer in Fellowship's *Journal*; Theosophical Publishing House for extracts from *The Hidden Wisdom in the Holy Bible* by Geoffrey Hodson, from *Man Incarnate* by P. D. and L. J. Bendit, and from *The Wheel of Rebirth* by H. K. Challoner; Watkins Publishing House for extract from *The Bhagavad Gita* translated by Charles Johnston.

The author also wishes to thank Roger Evans, Director of the Institute for Psychosynthesis for advice about quotations from *Psychosynthesis* by Robert Assagioli, published by Hobbs, Dorman & Co. Inc., New York, 1965.

Forbearance is asked if the author has overlooked, or failed to trace, any source from which permission to quote ought to have been sought.

*   *   *

Biblical quotations are from either the Revised or Authorised Versions of the Bible.

Personal Introduction

'Of making many books there is no end, and much study is a weariness of the flesh.'[1]

In the light of this observation, which must be at least as true today as it was when it was written nearly 3000 years ago, what is the justification for this book? Why has it been written? The answer involves a brief excursion into autobiography.

From an early age I was much concerned with whether human life had a purpose. I put the question to my parents but received replies which failed to satisfy. I then pressed the question – to their embarrassment and at some risk to family harmony! My mother was a quite splendid person holding orthodox Christian beliefs. What began to worry me – I was then in my teens – were the Buddhists and Hindus. What made us so sure that we (Christians) were right, and that they (Buddhists and Hindus) were wrong? By now I had developed a keen interest in the paranormal, and on going up to Cambridge I met, and came to know well, Professor C. D. Broad who was then President of the Society for Psychical Research. At the same time there began a life long friendship with Dr Chandra D. S. Gooneratne, a mature student from Sri Lanka who was deeply versed in Eastern religious literature. These two interlocking interests – in the paranormal, and in religious literature, both Christian and non-Christian – constituted the starting point, and have since provided the framework, for my continuing concern with the question which I asked my parents many years ago, 'What is the purpose of human life?'

Today I sense that there is an increasing number of

people, especially young people, who are asking this question and who are finding the current answers at best incomplete and at worst unacceptable. *It is for people such as these that this book has been written.* It is not a work of scholarship as that word is normally understood, since in spite of a lifelong interest in comparative religion, philosophy, and psychical research, I am in no sense a professional in any of these subjects. The object of this book is to focus attention on matters concerning the purpose of life and the nature of man, and to suggest certain avenues, the exploring of which may prove helpful and illuminating.

Halfway through the last century very few people had time and capacity to think and ponder. For the great majority providing the necessities of life was a full-time and all-embracing occupation. It is easy to be misled by historical novels about people who led interesting lives of considerable culture. Such people there were indeed, but they constituted a very small proportion of the whole. A book such as Trevelyan's *English Social History*[2] leaves no doubt about the kind of lives led by the great majority. By today's standards, at least in Western societies, hours of work, whether in the factory or on the land, were unbelievably long and conditions of work more often than not incredibly bad.

Science as we know it today was in its infancy, and the number of people who were both literate and numerate was very small. The result was an age that was authoritative, for if one had not the time to think and ponder there was little alternative but to accept the authority of those who had. And this applied to thought as well as action.

Today most people in Western societies have time to think and ponder if they so desire. Most people in these societies are, at least in some measure, both literate and numerate, and science has developed beyond all recognition. The extent to which an unconscious appreciation of the scientific method – the name given to the three-fold process of collecting the facts, making an informed guess as to what will

2

explain the facts, and checking the guess by observations or appropriately designed experiments – has spread throughout society I believe to be particularly significant. As a result of the increasingly vital part played by science in ordinary life, everyone realises that science is important. There follows the inevitable question 'How is it that science has achieved so much?' The answer is to be found in the third stage of the scientific method – 'Checking the guess by appropriately designed experiments.' Does the guess work?

A questioning attitude of mind 'Does it work?' has now permeated the whole of Western style society and is fundamental to an understanding of our situation today. It applies, moreover, to the whole of life – to religion, education, politics, industry – not just to matters scientific. Before the war this was not the case. For most of us there existed areas surrounded by notices such as 'Private', 'Keep out', 'Trespassers will be prosecuted'! These areas contained and often concealed our most cherished prejudices, assumptions and presuppositions – mental and psychological frameworks which were regarded as unchanging and immune from examination. Now nothing is too sacrosanct to be questioned. People, especially young people, are no longer prepared to accept authoritative statements unless they can be seen to be based on experience, on what is seen to work.

As a result of this questioning, an age of authority is passing away and with it are disappearing many cherished beliefs and practices which cannot stand up to the questions: Are they founded on what happens in practice? Can I test them from my own experience? Do they work? Concurrently with this are the tremendous successes which science has had in explaining a vast range of phenomena in terms of physics and chemistry. The upshot of these two developments is the prevalent very widely held view that, given time, everything will be explicable in terms of physics and chemistry, including life itself. Under such circumstances it is not surprising that 'Let us eat, drink and be merry for tomorrow we die' should be the philosophy of life in practice, if not in theory, of very many. But as a philosophy of life it is self-defeating, even barbaric – by which the Greeks meant non-understanding of worthwhile things – because concern with one's own wants and desires irrespective of the wants and desires of others invariably leads to unhappiness and, if pushed far enough, to disaster.

In this book I have gone to many different sources and drawn on many different traditions. No claim is made for any kind of authority. If what is said rings true, good. If it does not, the book should be returned to the shelf. But what is said or suggested should not be rejected simply because it is unfamiliar.

The book is in four Parts. Chapters 1 and 2 formulate the problem. Chapters 3 to 5 set out the evidence. Chapters 6 to 10 are concerned with what the evidence indicates. Chapters 11 to 15 discuss the implications.

In all relevant contexts throughout this book it will be assumed that 'he' includes 'she'.

References

1. Ecclesiastes, 12:12
2. *English Social History: A survey of six centuries. Chaucer to Queen Victoria.* G. M. Trevelyan. (Longmans, Green & Co. 1942. Penguin 1964)

Part I
The Quest

1: Education – For What?

We live in an age of perfect means and confused ends.

Albert Einstein

Today we have the knowledge, skill and experience to reach the moon, but we still lack the wisdom to inherit the earth.[1]

Lincoln Ralphs

The West is a civilisation without a philosophy and is rotting at the core because of this. Happy is he we are told, who doubles his standard of living every 25 years. More and more of the same for decade after decade? . . . Of course, things to be consumed are delightful in themselves and everyone should have what he needs of them; but man treated as worker-consumer, however fat his wage-packet or salary cheque, is man without dignity, manipulated man, degraded man, frustrated man, alienated man.[2]

James Hemming

So much has been written about education during the last twenty-five years that the reader would be justified in asking whether there could be anything worth saying that has not already been said. In answer to such a question, it can be pointed out that most of what has been said or written relates to method, to answering 'How?' Much less has been concerned with aim, to answering 'Why? To what end?' It is with certain aspects of the second of these two questions that this book is primarily concerned.

One of Plato's dialogues contains the following advice: 'Before embarking on a philosophical discussion, define your terms and clarify your concepts.' Let us now do just this – for education.

7

According to Webster, education is 'the impartation or acquisition of knowledge, skill, or development of character, as by study or discipline'. Its derivation is: *educare* – to train; *educere* – to draw out. To the question 'Is a child or young person to be regarded as a bottle to be filled or a candle to be lit?',[3] the dictionary and derivation answer 'Both'. But in practice, as distinct from theory, the emphasis in much secondary and tertiary education continues to be on the acquisition of information – 'The bottle to be filled.' To educate: 'Why? To what end?' At a superficial level the reply is clear enough: 'For the benefit of the individual concerned and of the community of which he or she is a member.' But, probing a little deeper, of what does the benefit consist, and how is it measured? The second question raises acute difficulties because the benefits are not in general quantifiable. To the first question there seem to be four answers. It should enable the individual concerned:

(a) To provide for himself and his family the basic necessities of life – food, clothing, shelter and security – and to play his part in satisfying the corresponding needs of the community.

(b) To appreciate, and to contribute to, contemporary culture[4] – defined by Webster as 'the characteristic attainments of a people or social order' – and to influence the development of that culture towards ever more noble ends.

(c) To evolve and formulate guide lines for living, i.e. a philosophy of life. To be able to distinguish between wisdom, knowledge and dogma; between what is permissible and what is advisable; between what is expedient and what is right.

(d) To develop and realise his full potentialities as a member of the human family, remembering always (i) that humanity is but a part of the stream of life and, on a geological time scale, a relative newcomer, and (ii) that many species have evolved and been extinguished because they evolved along lines which were inappropriate to some long term goal.

Over the years attitudes to what would be called today tertiary education have altered greatly, and it is instructive to note the changes in emphasis which have occurred in Western Europe since the founding of the earliest universities – Bologna, Paris, and Oxford – in the thirteenth century. This was a time when universities sponsored 'religious and useful learning'. Bologna was famous for law, Paris for medicine, and Oxford for theology. The university was a microcosm of society. And society, like its universities, was organised with a Christian vision and perspective. A university was a compact society, training men not only for life, but for death as well. Men were instructed, not only in knowledge but also in skills; and doctors, lawyers and clergy were supplied to meet the needs of society and the Church. Such was the picture of a university in the thirteenth century and for some centuries afterwards. As Christopher Dawson remarks, 'The intellectual synthesis of the thirteenth century was the crowning completion of centuries of continuous effort to achieve an integration of the religious doctrine of the Christian Church with the intellectual tradition of ancient culture.'[5]

This synthesis was indeed a great achievement, but, as always, the greater the achievement, the greater the danger of crystallisation. For life is not static; knowledge grows and experience widens. If crystallisation was to be avoided, it was essential for the synthesis to adapt to increasing knowledge and widening experience. But this did not happen. Instead, there developed a prescriptive theology which knew all the answers beforehand and became authoritative and definitive for the whole of intellectual life. It was a theology that gathered around itself all the humanities, and became a tree of knowledge which the universities existed to propagate throughout the length and breadth of the land. But like all neat and well rounded systems, this theological synthesis only preserved its polish and neatness by becoming steadily more detached from the society around it. The result was that by the beginning of the nineteenth century nothing but a travesty remained of the mediaeval integration of six centuries before. The notion

9

that university education should 'teach some temporal calling or some mechanical art, or some physical secret' was described by Newman as 'a fallacy'. The task of a university, said Newman, was rather to train gentlemen; to prepare man 'to fill any post with credit by exposing him to masterpieces of human thought and knowledge'. By the middle of the nineteenth century specialisation and fragmentation had replaced synthesis and integration. Stemming from the German thirst for *wissenschaft*, as exemplified by the universities of Berlin and Göttingen, the intellectual climate was characterised by the concept of knowledge for its own sake, with scant regard for its application; devotion to the purest of learning, entirely uncontaminated by the outside world, and to researches 'casting a fitful and intermittent light on non-existent problems'.[6] Small wonder that 'academic' tended to become a word of abuse! At the same time the effect of the scientific revolution initiated by Bacon, Harvey, Boyle and Newton, in the sixteenth and seventeenth centuries – a revolution in which British universities played a conspicuously small part – had led to a general sharpening of the critical faculty, and so to an undermining of dogmatism in general and of dogmatic theology in particular. A celebrated example of the latter followed the publication in 1859 of Darwin's *The Origin of Species by Means of Natural Selection*.

The next development was pioneered by the Continental Technische Hochschulen towards the end of the last century. This followed a realisation of the capacity of applied science to mould man's material environment, a realisation which led to the immense technological developments of the last one hundred years. Which brings us to today. What do we see?

> Society, far from being a compact whole, is now no more than a loose federation of groups, possessing and pursuing, for the most part, different goals, and our universities once again are microcosms of the world outside.[7]
>
> Ian Ramsey

10

EDUCATION – FOR WHAT?

When we anatomise British universities to discover what their purpose is we receive a mixed answer. There has been an accretion of functions over the centuries. From Bologna and Salerno comes the function of the university to train students for certain professions, like the church, medicine, and law. From Oxford and Cambridge comes the university's function as a nursery for gentlemen, statesmen, and administrators. From Göttingen and Berlin comes the function of the university as a centre for scholarship and research. From Charlottenburg and Zürich and Massachusetts comes the function of the university to be a staff college for technological experts and specialists. The cardinal problem facing universities today is how to reconcile these four different functions in one and the same institution. What is to be the long-term solution we simply do not know.[8]

Eric Ashby

In relation to the purpose of education formulated under (a) to (d) at the beginning of this chapter, contemporary education is much involved with (a), providing the basic necessities of life, but successively less concerned with (b), (c) and (d), cultural growth and developing a philosophy of life. Due to this lack of balance there is confusion and disenchantment. To the writer it seems that the need today is for a new synthesis, a return to what prevailed in the thirteenth century, but on a higher turn of the spiral. Is this developing? No. Or if it is, it is not very apparent. As to why not, the following extract from a hard hitting article by the Rev. Professor Schoneberg Setzer is singularly relevant:

Let us be painfully frank. Despite the fact that theological differences often testify to the rich diversity of man's experiences and creative interpretation, the bedlam and babel of irreconcilable dogmas is probably a scandal to any decent divine order that exists; and intelligent, educated men living today within the general ecumenicity of the natural sciences seem to sense this. Certainly they have a right to think lightly of theology until we get our house in order.

It is equally scandalous that science has learned so much about matter and such a little about mind. The only

11

epistemology used by most scientists is vectored for the control of gross physical nature, so that consequently it is not able to do justice to all of reality's dimensions. Research into altered states of consciousness, primary religious phenomena, psychic energy, and so forth, is miniscule in comparison to the huge effort – often redundant – in materialistic and physicalistic research. There has simply been little interest on the part of science in the great spiritual questions of human life. Religious concerns have often been callously dismissed as illusory panaceas, power politics and pathology. But if science is supposed to serve the whole man, it is indeed a scandal that a huge proportion of our civilization's human and material resources has been absorbed by a sub-culture which has systematically screened out the study of the transcendent and ultimately human.[9]

Where then do we go from here? To the writer it appears probable, if not inevitable, that any new synthesis will centre round the answers to two questions. What is the purpose of life on this planet? And what are the potentialities of the ordinary man or woman?

References

1. *Youth and its Responsibilities*, Sir Lincoln Ralphs, (*Journal of the Royal Society of Arts*, April 1976)
2. *The Humanist Signpost*, James Hemming, (*New Statesman*, 27 Oct. 1967)
3. The first reference to this phrase known to the writer occurred many years ago in a letter to *The Times* from a Mr David Baldin of the U.S.A.
4. A recent UNESCO document refers to culture as 'the sum total of a people's creative activities, its methods of production and of appropriation of material assets, its form of organisation, its beliefs and sufferings, its work and its leisure, its dreams and its successes'
5. *Religion and the Rise of Western Culture*, Christopher Dawson, (Sheed & Ward, 1950), p. 234
6. *Technology and the Academics*, Eric Ashby, (Macmillan & Co., 1958), p. 42

7. *Separation and Integration*, Ian Ramsey, Bishop of Durham, (Paper presented at U.T.G. Conference, Oxford, April 1968)
8. Same as ref. 6, p. 68
9. *Parapsychology and the Doctrine of God*, J. Schoneberg Setzer, (*Quarterly Journal Spiritual Frontiers Fellowship*, Vol. V, No. 3, Summer 1973)

2: Clearing the Ground

Another of the king's chief men went on to say: 'Your Majesty, when we compare the present life of man with that time of which we have no knowledge, it seems to me like the swift flight of a lone sparrow through the banqueting-hall where you sit in the winter months to dine with your thanes and counsellors. Inside there is a comforting fire to warm the room; outside, the wintry storms of snow and rain are raging. This sparrow flies swiftly in through one door of the hall, and out through another. While he is inside, he is safe from the winter storms; but after a few moments of comfort, he vanishes from sight into the darkness whence he came. Similarly, man appears on earth for a little while, but we know nothing of what went before this life, and what follows. Therefore if this new teaching can reveal any more certain knowledge, it seems only right that we should follow it.'[1]

Bede

Do not fear to be eccentric in opinion, for every opinion now accepted was once eccentric.[2]

Bertrand Russell

These are times of great decision, great threatening, and great disillusionment. The past order, the stability and the values which your generation took for granted, have now almost entirely collapsed as things to be taken for granted. The field of values can never be destroyed, but it has been eroded by the present agnosticism, doubt and cynicism. It is cynicism in high places that has destroyed the fabric of the life you knew.[3]

A Teacher

An essential or real change must begin in the individual; it has to be a change of heart, not superficial, and there is no

14

other solution for the present world problem. All that is being now attempted is merely to contain the problem as best one can. Man needs to discover himself behind the various masks of race, religion, nationality, and so forth. This discovery will lead man to truths that he needs to learn in the new age which is opening.[4]

N. Sri Ram

Before we start to examine the two fundamental questions raised at the end of the preceding chapter, there are certain matters which warrant attention.

The importance of keeping an open mind

Man is so constituted that what seems incredible when first developed or discovered is accepted without thought and as a matter of course within a strikingly short space of time. Examples are legion: motor cars, aeroplanes, telephones, wireless, television, to name but a few. Initial reaction to these inventions was amazement verging on unbelief. Now, their existence is so completely taken for granted that any suggestion of their possible disappearance would be greeted with consternation. Yet these developments have all taken place within the last one hundred years. Though these examples are all concrete, at more abstract levels the position is not dissimilar. Take the aether for example. Towards the end of the last century its existence was generally accepted. Now it is regarded as an exploded myth. As another illustration of how rapidly views change, reflect on the concept of matter. A century ago matter was thought to consist of exceedingly small indivisible particles. Fifty years later each particle had become a kind of miniature solar system. And now? The solar system model has been shown to be inadequate and been replaced by . . . ? Difficult to say![5] The time taken for some firmly held concept to be discarded and to be replaced by another is remarkably short. Yet man's make-up is such that at any given moment, what is asserted, whether concrete or abstract, tends to be regarded as the last word. In one sense it is. But so often there is a failure to appreciate that though it is the last word when spoken, the story is only just beginning, and there are many many more words still to come. A realisation of this fact leads to an open mind and to humility, and with humility come the thought provoking attitudes of awe and wonder. There are so many things in life that we take for granted, but the understanding and significance of which remain mysteries. Seeing, for instance. The impulses are quantitative; sight is qualitative. How can something that is quantitative be transformed into something that is qualitative? The same applies to hearing, taste, touch and smell; or consider existence – that people and things are. To reflect on this amidst the beauty of the countryside on a summer evening or under the stars on a brilliant night in winter is salutary, and a good corrective for intellectual arrogance.

The realisation that life is lived on the basis of probabilities.

Regarding the future, even the immediate future, very few things are absolutely certain. Some years ago a relative started to cross a road with the implicit expectation that he would reach the other side. But this eminently reasonable assumption was not fulfilled. He collapsed with an acute attack of lumbago when halfway across and was removed in an ambulance! The only proof there is that a mountain can be climbed and the summit reached is to undertake the climb and to get to the top. No amount of argument can prove *in advance* that the attempt will be successful. Apart from the inevitability of death of the physical body, absolute proof or certainty is hard to come by outside the realms of logic and of pure mathematics. Hence the phrase, so essential to the law, 'proved beyond reasonable doubt'. Appraising probabilities, albeit done for the most part quite unconsciously, is an inescapable concomitant of normal living.

An appreciation of the scope and limitations of science.

So long as we are concerned with phenomena or

16

happenings the occurrence or non-occurrence of which is normal, no new problems arise; that is, no problems of which the existence is not already known. But what are we to think when confronted with phenomena or happenings, alleged or observed, the existence of which is not normal? Such events are in the main of two kinds. Of one kind are abnormal events which are not inconsistent with scientific laws as at present formulated, e.g. a man 7½ ft tall; or a rainfall (in U.K.) of four inches in twenty-four hours. Such events, though often interesting, are not necessarily significant. Of the other kind are abnormal events which appear to be inconsistent with current scientific laws, for example telepathy, or the bending of forks and spoons by non-physical means.[6] Events of this kind may be very important indeed. If their existence is confirmed, it may indicate that the contemporary framework of Western scientific thought requires amendment.[7]

Phenomena or happenings which appear to be inconsistent with current scientific laws belong in turn to one of two categories. Those which can be reproduced at will by suitably designed experiments, and those which can not. Events in the first category are susceptible to what are usually referred to as the three stages of the scientific method. Stage one, collecting the relevant data, i.e. the observed facts; stage two, framing an hypothesis, i.e. making an informal guess as to what will explain the facts; stage three, testing the validity of the hypothesis, i.e. the guess, by appropriately designed experiments or statistical techniques. From events within this category at the time of their discovery has evolved the whole fabric of modern science. But what is to be our attitude to events in the second category, to events which cannot be reproduced at will by suitably designed experiments or statistical techniques, such as cases involving precognition. Though not susceptible to investigation by the scientific method as at present practised, such events may be highly significant. An illustrative example of the scientific method is given in Appendix I.

17

Before attempting to answer this question it is pertinent to consider the scope and limitations of science. Science is derived from the Latin word *scientia*, and is defined in the Oxford Dictionary as 'systematised knowledge'. Now knowledge which can be systematised must have certain characteristics. It must either be such as can be measured in some way – of this kind of knowledge Eddington says in one of his books that it is ultimately reducible to 'pointer readings'; the natural sciences such as chemistry, physics, mechanics, geology, meteorology, astronomy, all have this characteristic – or, if not reducible to purely quantitative treatment, it must be classifiable, in some such way as patterns of behaviour can be classified. The human sciences such as anthropology, sociology, psychology, are all concerned with knowledge of this kind. Occupying a position between the natural and human sciences are the biological sciences such as zoology, microbiology, human biology. Two questions now spring to mind. First, how does science progress, and what is the standing of a scientific law? Second, what, if anything, lies outside the scope of science?

To a greater or lesser extent all scientists proceed by applying to their problems 'the scientific method', the name given to the threefold process already referred to. But it is important to notice that science does not evolve in only one direction. Besides the discoveries which underlie the technological developments which are so rapidly transforming our material environment, there is the constant struggle to diminish the number of fundamental concepts. Not so long ago magnetism and electricity were regarded as wholly unconnected. We know now that this is not the case. But what of gravity and electromagnetism? Are these wholly independent?

As science progresses, laws are formulated, for example Newton's Laws of Motion; the First and Second Laws of Thermodynamics. Law used in this sense is applied to a hypothesis which has been so extensively tested as to dispel all doubt about its essential correctness within a prescribed range of conditions: Newton's Laws of Motion for example. With all respect to a leading daily paper which referred to some of Einstein's discoveries under the heading 'Newton proved all wrong', there is no doubt that Newton's Laws of Motion and other 'Laws'that contemporary science accepts are, and will continue to be, sufficiently accurate for most ordinary purposes. 'Truth successively takes shape, each grade above its last presentment' says Browning. Expressed more prosaically, truth is approached by a process of successive approximation.

To answer the question: 'What, if anything, lies outside the scope of science?' we have only to consider some questions based on those formulated by Macneile Dixon in *The Human Situation*.[8]

Does science help us to write *Hamlet*, to paint the *Mona Lisa*, or to compose 'The Pastoral Symphony'? I do not think so. What has science to say when she is asked to explain compassion, the mystic's thirst for God, or sacrifice for an ideal, if need be unto death? She is silent. Turning to quite homely matters. Does science help us to arrange a bowl of flowers or choose a dress? I doubt it. And what about the magic and mystery of love?

These questions and the answers to them show quite clearly that vast areas of life lie, and in the foreseeable future will continue to lie, outside the realm of science. Science, as at present defined, is concerned with phenomena or happenings which can be measured or classified, and with answering the question 'How?', or 'Why?' when used in the sense of 'How?'. For investigating such phenomena or happenings science has evolved the scientific method. With phenomena or happenings which cannot be measured or classified, and with questions relating to purpose (or why when related to purpose) science has little or no concern. Between these two areas lies a no-man's-land of vast extent and interest. In this area lie the abnormal events already referred to which are only in part measurable or classifiable and which cannot be reproduced at will by suitably designed experiments. For this very reason the investigation of such events has often been looked on askance. But today, with a better appreciation of the limitations and scope of science and a growing realisation of the significance of some of these events, attitudes are changing. The approach to such events can be broadly that of the scientific method, but with the three stages much more loosely defined, especially stage three – testing the hypothesis by appropriately designed experiments. At each stage a qualitative element will enter in, and seldom will it be possible to arrive at the conclusion 'proved beyond reasonable doubt'. Indicated with some degree of probability will be a much more frequent outcome. Although it may be impossible to arrange for a certain kind of event to happen under prescribed conditions, the fact that such events have occurred on many different occasions may constitute evidence of a very powerful nature. If an event has only happened once or twice, all sorts of special factors such as coincidence, inaccurate reporting, or deliberate fraud, may be adduced as explanation. But if the event is known to have happened many times, the picture changes under the weight of cumulative evidence.

An appreciation of how, in practice, most scientific discoveries are made.[9]

Most scientific text books give the impression that their subject has developed logically step by step from some clearly defined starting point. In practice this simply isn't true. The second stage of the scientific method – framing an hypothesis, i.e. making a guess as to what will explain a whole range of previously uncorrelated phenomena is not a matter of logical reasoning, of proceeding from the general to the particular, but of induction, of going from the particular to the general. This calls for quite different qualities of mind. Reasoning plays a part no doubt, but so too do imagination and intuition,[10] two qualities not easily defined. Many engineers and scientists would agree with Professor George King when he says 'I am familiar with the

20

absolute necessity of intuition for making any other than pedestrian advances in science and technology'. In a similar vein Sir Peter Medawar has said that scientific hypotheses cannot and do not arise from purely inductive reasoning. Inductive reasoning has its uses, but is simply not capable of adding that essential comprehension which turns a collection of observations into a meaningful ordered synthesis. Having hit upon his synthesis by other means, the scientist does not usually feel any need to explain that this has happened, but proceeds to write down a series of reasoned steps that could have brought him to the conclusions which he did in fact reach.

A famous example of the qualities called into play is Kekule's description of his discovery of the structure of benzene:

> I was sitting, writing at my text book; but the work did not progress; my thoughts were elsewhere. I turned my chair to the fire and dozed. Again the atoms came gambolling before my eyes. This time the smaller groups kept modestly in the background. My mental eye, rendered more acute by repeated visions of the kind, could now distinguish larger structures, of manifold conformation: long rows, sometimes more closely fitted together; all twining and twisting in snake-like motion. But look! What was that? One of the snakes had seized hold of its own tail, and the form whirled mockingly before my eyes. As if by a flash of lightning I awoke; and I spent the rest of the night in working out the consequences of the hypothesis.[9]

Six of the atoms had arranged themselves into a ring – the benzene ring – and immediately Kekule realised that the problem had been solved.

Although the preceding example of intuition, of immediate apprehension, is in the field of science, the faculty is a quite general one and may manifest at any time and under almost any conditions. Moreover, what is disclosed to the understanding is almost invariably accompanied by a conviction of its truth. But in view of the number of mutually inconsistent convictions which their possessors claim to be the result of intuition, it is as well to sound a note of caution. Kekule again: 'Let us learn to dream, gentlemen, then perhaps we shall find the truth . . . but let us beware of publishing our dreams before they have been put to the proof by the waking understanding.'[10] Reason and intuition are like two rails, each essential for smooth running on life's journey.

Current views about the purpose of human life on this planet.

Views about the purpose of human life on this planet range from total pessimism – that human life is completely devoid of long term purpose, to considerable optimism – that humanity has ahead of it no mean destiny. The following are examples of a pessimistic outlook –

(i) Life's but a walking shadow, a poor player
That struts and frets his hour upon the stage
And then is heard no more; it is a tale
Told by an idiot, full of sound and fury,
Signifying nothing.[11]

Macbeth

(ii) That Man is the product of causes which had no prevision of the end they were achieving; that his origin, his growth, his hopes and fears, his loves and his beliefs, are but the outcome of accidental collocations of atoms; that no fire, no heroism, no intensity of thought and feeling, can preserve an individual life beyond the grave; that all the labours of the ages, all the devotion, all the inspiration, all the noonday brightness of human genius, are destined to extinction in the vast death of the solar system, and that the whole temple of Man's achievement must inevitably be buried beneath the debris of a universe in ruins – all these things, if not quite beyond dispute, are yet so nearly certain, that no philosophy which rejects them can hope to stand. Only within the scaffolding of these truths, only on the firm foundation of unyielding despair, can the soul's habitation henceforth be safely built.[12]

Bertrand Russell

of an optimistic attitude –

> (iii) I have said, ye are gods, and all of you are children of the most High.
>
> Psalm 82
>
> (iv) Take courage for the race of man is divine.
>
> Pythagoras

The need for a new metaphysic.

So much of what is going on in this country today is separative and divisive. We see it in every walk of life.[13] And this is sad because it means that nervous energy, one of our most precious possessions, is being squandered on internal conflict instead of being used creatively. Why is this? How can such energy be channelled into more constructive ends?

There are in the dictionary two very important words beginning with 'r' – *rights* and *responsibilities*. The emphasis today is all on *rights*; *responsibilities* are rarely referred to. If every member of this country – rich or poor, of high estate or low – were to spend as much time thinking about his responsibilities as about his rights, conditions would be transformed overnight. All that is required is a change in attitude of mind.[14] Moreover, such a change would promote happiness. Increasing emphasis on *my rights* inclines to an inturned attitude of mind from which stem boredom and dissatisfaction. Whereas increasing emphasis on *my responsibilities* inclines to an outgoing attitude of mind from which spring interest and satisfaction. That the world can be made a better place by altering conditions without altering attitudes of mind is a fundamental and widespread fallacy. This becomes apparent as soon as it is noted that changing conditions without a corresponding change in attitude of mind merely replaces one set of evils by another. 'In capitalism man has been exploited by man; in communism it is the other way round.'

Though attitudes of mind present a continuous spectrum about which it is dangerous to generalise, it is none the less true that the outlook of an individual or group tends to be one of crude self-interest, or of enlightened self-interest, or of selfless concern for the well-being of the whole. What is striking is that almost everyone, if asked, would agree that the widespread adoption of the last of the three attitudes of mind just mentioned – a selfless concern for the well-being of the whole – would go far to solve our present problems. Yet, attitudes remain unaltered. In practice little happens.

In *The Human Situation*[8] Professor Macneile Dixon refers to a situation in which a little girl asked her mother 'But, Mummy, why should I be good when I want to be naughty?', a question which professional philosophers have found some difficulty in answering. Replacing the little girl by an ordinary man or woman the question becomes 'Why should I concern myself with the well-being of the whole when all that I am interested in is the well-being of myself and my immediate family and friends? Why should I?' And that is the nub of the problem.

What makes a group of people work together? The answer usually is either a common fear or a common faith; or, may be, a combination of the two. This is well illustrated by the Second World War when the nation was united to an extent that it has certainly not been since. We were united by a common fear voiced by Churchill in his unforgettable words 'If we don't hang together we shall certainly hang separately', and by a common faith 'Freedom is in peril defend it with your might'. Is there a common fear or common faith which could unite the nation today in a manner analogous to that in which it was united during the Second World War?

Let us begin with fear. Is there anything today which warrants universal fear? It would seem that inaction in the face of poverty, pollution, violence and the arms race comes into this category. On 9th May 1969 U Thant, when opening a conference on the Second Development Decade, rivetted his audience by saying:

CLEARING THE GROUND

I do not wish to seem overdramatic, but I can only conclude from the information that is available to me as Secretary-General that the Members of the United Nations have perhaps ten years left in which to subordinate their ancient quarrels and launch a global partnership to curb the arms race, to improve the human environment, to defuse the population explosion, and to supply the required momentum to world development efforts. If such a global partnership is not forged within the next decade, then I very much fear that the problems I have mentioned will have reached such staggering proportions that they will be beyond our capacity to control.

Since then a dispassionate study of the literature shows that the problems are real and getting worse. During the past few years they have been the subject of much publicity and many talks. But what is actually being done? That action must be preceded by discussion is obvious, but it is essential that talking should lead to doing – for two reasons. First, discussion which does not lead to action is psychologically enervating; the subject loses freshness and becomes stale. Second, unless we do something about poverty, pollution, violence and the arms race, they will do something to us.[15] If words are to be followed by action, sacrifice will be necessary; sacrifice of money, time and may be prestige.[16] But is there the necessary will?[17] That is the crucial question.

So much for a common fear. Have we a common faith?

Prior to Galileo looking through his telescope, the Christian metaphysic had held undisputed sway throughout Western Europe for many centuries. Galileo's suggestion that the earth went round the sun, and not vice versa, had little to do with religion but the ecclesiastical hierarchy of that time thought that it had and strenuously opposed it. Thus began a long and progressively serious conflict between increasing scientific knowledge and the Christian metaphysic as dogmatised at the various Church Councils.

For the writer the heart of religion is the insights which have been distilled by the great teachers in the crucible of

25

their own experience and then propounded in a form appropriate to the knowledge and understanding of the people amongst whom they lived. Though these psychological insights change little with time, this is not true of the philosophical and theological superstructure, the 'metaphysic' which is built around these insights. For the metaphysic must inevitably reflect the general outlook and state of scientific knowledge current at the time, and this does indeed change as the centuries go by. Today, largely due to the scientific discoveries of the last 150 years, the metaphysic which served so well in the past is no longer adequate and is in urgent need of recasting. Two areas of thought in which the need is particularly pressing are the purpose of life and the nature of man. What *is* the purpose of human life on this planet? What happens after death and before birth? Is death really the end and birth the beginning as scientific humanism, the dominant world view (in practice if not in theory) maintains? And what *are* the potentialities of the ordinary man or woman?

Dogmatic statements not susceptible to verification are no longer acceptable. Something more is looked for. But whatever the more may prove to be must be founded on experiment and experience. Any future metaphysic, to be effective, must provide convincing answers to these questions. If and when it does, it will go some way towards providing mankind with a common purpose.

Material development by itself cannot sustain our civilisation. It is fairly certain that without some acceptable alternative motive the old laws of survival will reassert their authority. To make life tolerable and indeed possible for intelligent man there must be some criterion of right and wrong, some positive motivation, some vision of an ideal, some beckoning inspiration. Without it we shall never get to grips with the population explosion, with racial prejudice, with starvation, with distribution of resources, with the conflicting demands of development and conservation, progress and pollution, or the control of the complex industrial communities and the liberties of the individual. Devising a new system or revising the existing one is a fairly daunting prospect. It will have to take into account everything known about the universe, the earth, ourselves and the existing industrial, commercial, legal and political structures. From this it must distil a theory which commands such a degree of acceptance that people will find the will to make it work, recognizing the need for the restraints it demands and the responsibilities and obligations it imposes.[18]

Duke of Edinburgh

Our situation now resembles that of a climber who has selected his peak, considered the difficulties, taken stock of his resources, and must now start the climb. The first stage of the climb is collecting and sifting relevant data. This is the subject matter of Part II.

References

1. *A History of the English Church and People*, Bede, Chap. 13
2. The seventh of Russell's Ten Commandments. The complete list is given in Appendix II
3. See Chapter 6 of *A Forgotten Truth*, D. M. A. Leggett & M. G. Payne, (Pilgrims Book Services, 1986)
4. *The Present World Crisis*, N. Sri Ram, (*Theosophical Journal*, Vol. 10, No. 1, 1969)
5. See *The Tao of Physics*, Fritjof Capra, (Wildwood House, 1975)
6. See *The Metal-Benders*, J. B. Hasted, (Routledge & Kegan Paul, 1981)
7. An excellent appraisal of the current situation is contained in *Parapsychology and the Nature of Life*, John L. Randall, (Souvenir Press, 1975)
8. *The Human Situation*, W. Macneile Dixon, (Edward Arnold & Co., 1946. First published 1937)
9. *Intuition*, G. B. Blaker, (*Radionic Quarterly*, June 1976), p. 26
10. See *An Essay on the Psychology of Invention in the Mathematical Field*, J. S. Hadamard, (Princeton University Press, Princeton, 1945)
11. *Macbeth*, Shakespeare, Act V, Scene V

12. *Philosophical Essays*, Bertrand Russell, (Longmans, Green & Co., 1910), 'The Free Man's Worship', p. 60
13. See *The Dilemma of Democracy*, Lord Hailsham, (Collins, 1978), Chap. III
14. When Guildford Cathedral was under construction, a story has it that a visitor asked three of the workmen what they were making. The first one replied – £20 a week; the second one – a wall; the third one – a great cathedral
15. See (i) *The Seventh Enemy*, Ronald Higgins, (Hodder & Stoughton, 1978), Parts one and two. (ii) *North South*. Report of the Brandt Commission, (Pan Books, 1980)
16. *Only One Earth – The Care and Maintenance of a Small Planet*, Barbara Ward and Rene Dubos, (Penguin Books, 1972)
17. *A World Divided*, Alexander Solzhenitsyn, (Address given at the 1978 Harvard Commencement Ceremony)
18. From the Oration given by The Duke of Edinburgh at King's College, London, December 1969

Part II
Evidence

3: From Mysticism

Belief is no adequate substitute for inner experience.[1]

C. G. Jung

Although the chapter heading is Mysticism, we shall begin by reflecting on religion. What is religion? Stated briefly it is the life of the spirit; the intuitive recognition by man that he possesses a spiritual nature, and the extent to which he manifests that nature. And if this is religion, what are religions? They are ladders, the climbing of which leads to the life of the spirit. Religions are the product of religion, but they are not religion. Religion does not really consist in belief, or ritual, or even worship, as ordinarily understood and practised – though it will give rise to them. For though belief, ritual and worship express ideas about the things of the spirit and so spring from a spiritual background, they belong in large measure to the realms of emotion and of discursive intellect, whereas the life of the spirit lies behind the emotions and the discursive intellect at a deeper level of being.[2] It is stated in *The Voice of the Silence* that 'The mind is the slayer of the real',[3] i.e. the real cannot be encountered until the realms of the emotions and of the discursive intellect have been transcended.

Perhaps the relationship between religion and religions can be made clearer by an analogy. Consider an individual and the clothes which he or she is wearing. The relationship of the clothes to the individual's personality is similar to the relationship between religions and religion. That an individual's dress is in some measure an indication of the wearer's personality is clear; but that it is no more than an

31

indication is equally clear. This analogy is helpful, moreover, in showing how pointless it usually is in the case of a particular person to try and replace one set of dogmatic beliefs, or form of ritual, or mode of worship, by another. If a person's dress is suitable for his/her life and occupation, why try and alter it? If, on the other hand, someone comes to you and says 'My dress is stained and tattered. What am I to do?' The situation is different and the answering of that question is a privilege, an opportunity, and a responsibility. Another matter for which this analogy may be instructive is religious revivals and the so-called conversions to which they give rise. The question to be asked is: 'Are these conversions merely a change of dress, arising perhaps from some change of mood of the wearer; or are they indications of something fundamental, a deepening of the wearer's consciousness?'

Having defined religion in this way, what is the evidence that the definition is of something real, and is not just the result of imagination and wishful thinking? To this question three observations can be made by way of answer. First, so far as is known, there is no tribe, people or culture, past or present, which is totally without a religion of some kind.[4] Second, we have the teaching and authority of the founders of the great religions, in particular, Gautama Buddha and Jesus Christ. Third, there is the testimony of the mystics, irrespective of race, creed and period. It can, of course, be argued that the religions of primitive peoples may have little in common with religion as previously defined, and that the founders of the great religions lived a long time ago. But this is not true of mystical experience which is shared by so many people in so many different times and places and which is often such as to bring about a permanent change in attitude and outlook of the one who has had the experience. Moreover, such experience is in general quite consistent with what appears to have been taught by the founders of the great religions.

In her book *Practical Mysticism* Evelyn Underhill defines mysticism as 'The art of union with Reality. The mystic is a person who has attained that union in greater or less degree; or who aims at and believes in such attainment.'[5] With this definition in mind, the following are six examples. They have been drawn from a vast literature on the subject and originate from people of very different backgrounds. The actual experiences are clearly of greatly varying depth.

First, the Neoplatonic philosopher Plotinus:

> Those divinely possessed and inspired have at least the knowledge that they hold some greater thing within them, though they cannot tell what it is; from the movements that stir them and the utterances that come from them they perceive the power, not themselves, that moves them: in the same way, it must be, we stand towards the Supreme when we hold *nous pure* [defined by Webster as 'God regarded as the World Reason']; we know the Divine Mind within, that which gives Being and all else of that order: but we know, too, that other, know that it is none of these, but a nobler principle than anything we know as Being; fuller and greater; above reason, mind, and feeling; conferring these powers, not to be confounded with them.[6]

Next, the celebrated Christian mystic Ruysbroeck:

> When love has carried us above all things, above the light, into the Divine Dark, there we are transformed by the Eternal Word Who is the image of the Father; and as the air is penetrated by the sun, thus we receive in peace the Incomprehensible Light, enfolding us and penetrating us. What is this light, if it be not a contemplation of the Infinite and an intuition of Eternity? We behold that which we are, and we are that which we behold, because our being, without losing anything of its own personality, is united with the Divine Truth which respects all diversity.[7]

Now, three relatively recent examples selected from the cases described in Raynor Johnson's *Watcher on the Hills.*[8]

Case 12 (Miss I.W.):

> As I preamble, I think it necessary to say that at the time of this experience I was a non-church-goer, and still am; therefore I am not what is generally known as a religious person. The

experience is far beyond my command of words and loses so much in the telling.

In the earliest stages of a long convalescence, when my body was too weak to lift its head from the pillow, the dark and empty inertia in which I lay was filled with light. It did not come in a sudden blaze, but so gently that I scarcely knew when it came. Barriers were down; my aloneness had gone; I was at one with every living creature and thing. I knew that, despite almost overwhelming evidence to the contrary, a trinity of Truth, Beauty and Justice was the basis of life, and that 'somehow good would be the final goal of ill'. In that beautiful Biblical phrase I knew that 'underneath were the Everlasting Arms'.

The light – 'illumination' is a better word – went as gently as it came, and left me with a legacy of knowledge that is beyond the bounds of belief and faith. Though my subsequent life has not justified retention of the knowledge, it has not been withdrawn, and never will be, because, being eternal, it is linked with the eternal in me.

Case 14 (from *This Wondrous Way of Life* by Brother Mandus):
I remember now (and I am always recalling it) the greatest experience in my life, that vital moment when I was baptised by the Holy Spirit within. For one perfect second, unexpected, unheralded, and while I was doing a trivial task, my personal mind and body were fused in Light; a breathless unbearable Light-Perfection, as intense as the explosion of a flash of lightning within me . . . In this timeless second I knew a Love, Knowledge and Ecstasy transcending anything I could understand or describe. I was lifted into the midst of God, in whom all people, all worlds, and every created life or thing moved and had their being. Perfection! Had I been suffering from the worst mental or physical disease known to men, in that Light I should instantly have been made Whole.

In that moment I knew my Lord dwells within my own being, and within everyone else. In that one moment I knew the truth of His eternal reality, and that He is All, that my Father and I are One, that all people and the Father are One, and that we are all One with each other in spirit.

Case 15 (from *Recorded Illuminates* by Winslow Hall, M.D.):
B.E.B. is a middle-class Englishwoman of literary interests and occupation.

FROM MYSTICISM

I was 35 at the time of the experience. It happened thus: on April 13th 1905 at eight a.m. I was standing among pine trees looking out at the sky when suddenly the heavens opened, as it were, and caught me up. I was swept up and out of myself altogether into a flood of White Glory. I had no sense of time or place. The ecstasy was terrific while it lasted. It could have lasted only a minute or two. It went as suddenly as it came. I found myself bathed with tears, but they were tears of joy. I felt *One* with everything and everybody; and somehow *I knew* that what I had experienced was Reality and that Reality is Perfection.

I would like to add that no words seem to me able to convey a thousandth part of the depth and reality of that experience, even so far as my own taste of it has gone. I fancy all one's normal faculties are first fused and then transcended.

Finally, a personal experience of the author:

I was standing in a crowded business train at Waterloo when I became aware that some subtle alchemy was taking place within my being. My purely personal consciousness sank into the background, and I became a channel. Power flowed in and love radiated out. Nearly everyone around me looked tired and jaded, and few could be called attractive. Yet I loved them one and all. For the first time in my life I began to understand the meaning of compassion. I knew beyond all doubt that each and all contained a spark of the divine, a darkened spark perhaps, but one which would in due time shine forth in a blaze of glory. At Guildford I left the train and the spell was broken.

The above was how I described the experience at the time, now more than thirty years ago. The similarity with what follows is striking.

Extract from *The Christian Agnostic* by Leslie Weatherhead, (First published 1965):

For a few seconds only, I suppose, the whole compartment was filled with light. This is the only way I knew in which to describe the moment, for there was nothing to *see* at all . . . A most curious, but overwhelming sense possessed me and filled me with ecstasy. All men were shining and glorious beings who in the end would enter incredible joy . . . All this happened over fifty years ago but even now I can see myself in the corner of that dingy, third-class compartment with the feeble lights of inverted gas mantles overhead and the Vauxhall platforms outside. In a few moments the glory had departed – all but one curious, lingering feeling. I loved– everybody in that compartment.[9]

If it is now asked why mystical experience, experience of the transcendent, seems only to occur on isolated occasions, a further extract from the writings of Evelyn Underhill provides an interesting comment:

Transcendental genius obeys the laws which govern all other forms of genius, in being susceptible of culture: and, indeed, cannot develop its full powers without an educative process of some kind. This strange art of contemplation, which the mystic tends naturally to practise during the whole of his career – which develops step by step with his vision and his love – demands of the self which undertakes it the same hard dull work, the same slow training of the will, which lies behind all supreme achievement, and is the price of all true liberty. It is the want of such training – such 'supersensual drill' – which is responsible for the mass of vague, ineffectual, and sometimes harmful mysticism which has always existed: the dilute cosmic emotion and limp spirituality which hangs, as it were, on the skirts of the true seekers of the Absolute and brings discredit upon their science.[10]

Though descriptions of mystical experience vary widely, a large number refer to –
(a) transcendence – of the world of the five physical senses, and of space and time as normally understood.
(b) certainty – about the significance and reality of their experience.
(c) conviction that love and perfection underlie all that is.
(d) unity, at-one-ment.

In connection with (d), and the vexed question of at-one-ment – with what? – the following ostensible communication from an advanced soul is significant:

> Jupiter fell in love with Semele and he revealed himself to her as a man. She thought herself strong enough to meet him on his own level, to be loved by a god. So she demanded insolently that he should come to her in his full divine status. What happened? She withered away, was consumed by his fire . . .
> Too considerable a revelation of God would drive the most spiritual human being mad. The highly gifted mystic or yogi was never in his earthly life-time united with God. Actually, his little spark was blown on so that it became a tiny flame during the occasions he had mystical experiences. Only when the long journey through infinite time has been made, only when the human soul has been fully used for the purposes of Divine Imagination, and this soul is incomparably enriched by the strength of all the other souls in its Group, can it experience Union with Divine Imagination. To be on the level with God one has to become a god, and that full glory is not to be experienced by any human being.[11]

Bearing in mind the impossibility of explaining the more evolved in terms of the less evolved, for example of discursive thinking in terms of emotional feeling, or of emotional feeling in terms of physical sensing, the extreme difficulty which the mystic has in describing his experience in words is not surprising. Indeed, it would be surprising if it were otherwise. What is striking are the number,[12] nature,[13] and general consistency of the experiences of which those just described are typical.[14]

The rest of this chapter will be devoted to a consideration of the transcendental or mystical elements of the Near Death Experience (NDE). This is the name given to the experience which a person may have when he (or she) is clinically dead but from which state he subsequently recovers. During the last ten to fifteen years NDE has become the subject of serious study both here and in America, and several books have been written describing and analysing the results.[15] Several hundred cases have been investigated, and in many the person concerned has brought back some recollection of what he experienced. A striking feature of these accounts is their consistency. Details differ, but the broad picture is the same in nearly every case. So much so that it is possible to refer to a number of specific stages.

The first stage is leaving the physical body and a feeling of peace and well-being, a welcome relief from any pain. The individual then becomes aware that though his sight and hearing are unimpaired he is looking down at his physical body from a point outside it. These two stages correspond closely with the Out-of-Body experiences (OOB's) described in Chapter 5. But now comes a new development – the dim but growing awareness of 'a new reality' and a sense of floating through a long and dark tunnel at the end of which is a light. Though initially only a point, it gradually expands. What follows next is termed 'the core experience' and is only the experience of some. Emerging from the tunnel into brilliantly lighted surroundings of great beauty the individual becomes aware of a presence or 'being of light'. At the behest of this presence the individual then reviews his life, very rapidly but in considerable detail.

At this stage, he has no awareness of time or space, and the concepts themselves are meaningless. Neither is he any longer identified with his body. Only the mind is present and it is weighing – logically and rationally – the alternatives that confront him at this threshold separating life from death: to go further into this experience or to return to earthly life. Usually the individual decides to return on the basis, not of his own preference, but on the perceived needs of his loved ones, whom his death would necessarily leave behind. Once the decision is made, the experience tends to be abruptly terminated.[16]

If the core experience so described is 'heavenly', it should be mentioned in fairness that a few individuals, fortunately very few, undergo an experience which can only be described as 'hellish'. In view of what is suggested in

Chapter 8, p. 115, a feature of some interest is that the phrases 'ascending to heaven' and 'descending to hell' may not be *wholly* figurative. *À propos* of the 'location' of the hellish experiences Rawlings says 'In most cases, this place seems to be underground or within the earth in some way.'[17] By the same token the 'location' of the other 'place' appears to be above the earth.

What is very significant about people who have had an NDE is that in almost every case fear of death is greatly diminished and belief in survival much increased.[18] And in most cases the experience gives rise to a fundamental change in outlook. For example:

> I always thought about social status and wealth symbols as the most important things in life until life was suddenly taken from me. Now I know that none of these are important. Only the love you show others will endure or be remembered. The material things won't count. Our present life is nothing compared to what you'll see later.[19]

More generally, Margot Grey has this to say:

> The obvious transformation that comes about in the lives of near-death survivors that have had a core experience tends to be both dramatic and profound. To the person who has experienced the subjectively undeniable view of the beauty of the cosmos and gained the understanding that one is an indissoluble part of that splendour, it would seem that the prime purpose of returning to physical life is to gain an opportunity to try to live life in accordance with the knowledge obtained while on the threshold of death.[20]

References

1. *The Undiscovered Self*, C. G. Jung. Translated by R. F. C. Hull, (Routledge & Kegan Paul, 1958), p. 37
2. See *The Gnosis or Ancient Wisdom in the Christian Scriptures*, William Kingsland, (George Allen & Unwin, 1937), Chap. 1
3. *The Voice of the Silence*, H. P. Blavatsky, Fragment I, verses 4, 5

4. In his *Notes Towards The Definition of Culture*, T. S. Eliot puts it this way: 'The first important assertion is that no culture has appeared or developed except together with a religion; according to the point of view of the observer, the culture will appear to be the product of the religion or the religion the product of the culture.'
   See also Chap. III of *The Divine Flame* by Sir Alister Hardy.

5. *Practical Mysticism*, Evelyn Underhill, (J. M. Dent & Sons, 1914), p. 3

6. *A History of Western Philosophy*, Bertrand Russell, (George Allen & Unwin, 1946), p. 313

7. *Rational Mysticism*, William Kingsland, (George Allen & Unwin, 1924), p. 279

8. *Watcher on the Hills*, Raynor C. Johnson, (Hodder & Stoughton, 1959), Chap. 3

9. *The Christian Agnostic*, Leslie D. Weatherhead, (Hodder & Stoughton, 1965), p. 40

10. *Mysticism*, Evelyn Underhill, (Methuen & Co., 4th edition, 1912), p. 359

11. Same as ref. 8, p. 105

12. In *Reports of ecstatic, paranormal or religious experience in Great Britain and the United States*, David Hay and Ann Morley, (Religious Experience Research Unit, Manchester College, Oxford, 1977), it is stated that 'Rather more than a third of all adults give a positive response to the question: "Have you ever been aware of, or influenced by, a presence or power?" '

13. See *The Medium, the Mystic, and the Physicist*, Lawrence LeShan, (Turnstone Press, 1974. First published 1966)

14. See *This Time-Bound Ladder*, (1977), and other publications, (Religious Experience Research Unit, Manchester College, Oxford)

15. See under 'Near Death Experiences' in Bibliography

16. *Life at Death*, Kenneth Ring, (Coward, McCann & Geoghegan, New York, 1980), p. 102

17. *Beyond Death's Door*, Maurice Rawlings, (Sheldon Press, 1979), p. 102

18. *Survival*, David Lorimer, (Routledge & Kegan Paul, 1984), p. 262
19. Same as ref. 17, p. 90
20. *Return from Death*, Margot Grey, (Arkana, 1985), p. 194

4: From Poetry

To believe life an irremediable disaster, the heavens and earth an imbecility, is to my way of thinking hard indeed. Since I am not prepared to believe the world a misery-go-round, a torture-chamber, a furnace of senseless affliction; since I am not prepared to believe the fiery, invincible soul a by-blow, a lamentable accident; I prefer to put my trust in the larger vision of the poets. To fortify our minds it is to them we have to return, and yet again return. They alone have understood. 'It exceeds all imagination to conceive,' wrote Shelley, 'what would have been the moral condition of the world if the poets had never been born . . . What were our consolations on this side of the grave, and what were our aspirations beyond it – if poetry did not ascend to bring light and fire from those eternal regions where the owl-winged faculty of calculation dare not ever soar?'[1]

W. Macneile Dixon

Why poetry? Because of what A.E. (George Russell) expresses so clearly in the following extract from *Song and its Fountains*:[2]

Let no one assume that I claim for even their highest utterance that infallibility which those who do not desire to think ask from their teachers, but it is through the poets and musicians alone that we get the sense of a glory transmitted from another nature, and as we mingle our imagination with theirs we are exalted and have the heartache of infinite desire. Truth for us cannot be in statements of ultimates but in an uplifting of our being, in which we are raised above ourselves and know that we are knocking at the door of the Household of Light. The poets and the great masters of music are those who have the expectation of inspiration. They wait upon the gods though they may not know when they turn inward in reverie what being it is upon whom they wait.

The rest of this chapter consists of quotations from the work of well-known poets. First, an extract from *Bishop Blougram's Apology* by Browning. This refers to the difficulty of maintaining a consistent attitude of unbelief in anything transcending the world of the five physical senses.

> And now what are we? Unbelievers both,
> Calm and complete, determinately fixed
> Today, tomorrow and for ever, pray?
> You'll guarantee me that? Not so, I think!
> In no wise! All we've gained is that belief,
> As unbelief before, shakes us by fits,
> Confounds us like its predecessor.
> Where's the gain? How can we guard our unbelief,
> Make it bear fruit to us? – the problem here.
> Just when we are safest, there's a sunset-touch,
> A fancy from a flower-bell, some one's death,
> A chorus-ending from Euripides,
> And that's enough for fifty hopes and fears
> As old and new at once as nature's self,
> To rap and knock and enter in our soul,
> Take hands and dance there, a fantastic ring,
> Round the ancient idol, on his base again,
> The grand Perhaps! We look on helplessly.
> There the old misgivings, crooked questions are –
> This good God, – what he could do, if he would,
> Would, if he could – then must have done long since:
> If so, when, where and how? Some way must be, –
> Once feel about, and soon or late you hit
> Some sense, in which it might be, after all.
> Why not, 'The Way, the Truth, the Life?'

The next two extracts suggest the possibility that life as lived now may provide the opportunity to atone for failings in a previous life.

> *Empedocles on Etna* (Act II)
> And then we shall unwillingly return
> Back to this meadow of calamity,

THE SACRED QUEST

This uncongenial place, this human life;
And in our individual human state
Go through the sad probation all again,
To see if we will poise our life at last,
To see if we will now at last be true
To our own only true, deep-buried selves,
Being one with which we are one with the whole world;
Or whether we will once more fall away
Unto some bondage of the flesh or mind,
Some slough of sense, or some fantastic maze
Forged by the imperious lonely thinking-power.

Matthew Arnold (1822–88)

Paracelsus. Scene 1.

At times I almost dream
I too have spent a life the sages' way
And tread once more familiar paths. Perchance
I perished in an arrogant self-reliance
Ages ago; and in that act, a prayer
For one more chance went up so earnest, so
Instinct with better light let in by death,
That life was blotted out – not so completely
But scattered wrecks enough of it remain,
Dim memories, as now, when seems once more
The goal in sight again . . .

Robert Browning (1812–89)

The four lines quoted from *Auguries of Innocence* show Blake to be a profound mystic. And in case what he says should be thought extravagant, it is significant that the late Mrs Bendit, a remarkable psychic, wrote, though not in poetry, in very similar vein.[3]

Auguries of Innocence

To see a World in a Grain of Sand,
And a Heaven in a Wild Flower,
Hold Infinity in the palm of your hand
And Eternity in an hour.

William Blake (1757–1827)

The next poem confirms what was said at the beginning of the chapter about the nature of true religion.

FROM POETRY

The Wise Years
(The monk, Lapidarius, in meditation)

Here, in this moorland cell, long years I strove,
To pierce the veil that hideth Heaven from man.
By fasts and vigils I wore thin the robe,
The fleshly robe that clogs the soul; in prayer
I from the body soared among the stars
And held high converse with the cherubim.
I moved in ecstasy, and all the land
Spake of my sainthood; people thronged from far
To gaze upon the man who walked with God.
Ah, little knew they! In my heart I wept,
For God was ever distant. Not with Him
I communed, but with fancies self-begot,
Half of sick brain and half of fevered flesh.

And then one eve – 'twas at the Lammastide
When every twilight is a taste of Heaven,
While half-distraught I laboured, sudden came
The light that shone on Paul; I caught my breath,
Felt on my forehead the cool hand of God,
And heard His holy accents in my ear:
'Why troublest thou thyself to mount to Me
When I am with thee always. Love My world,
The good green earth I gave thee for thy joy.'
Then through the rushes flowered the rose of eve,
And I went forth into the dewy air,
And made my first communion with God's world.

John Buchan (1875–1940)

The three poems which follow are commentaries on the mystery of life and are radiant with faith and hope.

The Dry Salvages

To explore the womb, or tomb, or dreams; all these are usual
Pastimes and drugs, and features of the press:
And always will be, some of them especially
When there is distress of nations and perplexity
Whether on the shores of Asia, or in the Edgware Road.
Men's curiosity searches past and future
And clings to that dimension. But to apprehend

THE SACRED QUEST

The point of intersection of the timeless
With time, is an occupation for the saint –
No occupation either, but something given
And taken, in a lifetime's death in love,
Ardour and selflessness and self-surrender.
For most of us, there is only the unattended
Moment, the moment in and out of time,
The distraction fit, lost in a shaft of sunlight,
The wild thyme unseen, or the winter lightning
Or the waterfall, or music heard so deeply
That it is not heard at all, but you are the music
While the music lasts. These are only hints and guesses,
Hints followed by guesses; and the rest
Is prayer, observance, discipline, thought and action.
The hint half guessed, the gift half understood, is Incarnation.

T. S. Eliot (1888–1965)

Beyond the Farthest Horizon

We have dreamed dreams beyond our comprehending,
Visions too beautiful to be untrue;
We have seen mysteries that yield no clue
And sought our goals on ways that have no ending.
We, creatures of the earth,
The lowly born, the mortal, the foredoomed
To spend our fleeting moments on the spot
Wherein tomorrow we shall be entombed
and hideously rot, –
We have seen loveliness that shall not pass;
We have beheld immortal destinies;
We have seen heaven and hell and joined their strife;
Ay, we whose flesh shall perish as the grass
Have flung the passion of the heart that dies
Into the hope of everlasting life.

Sidney Royse Lysaght (c. 1855–1941)

A Cosmic Outlook

On! I have guessed the end; the end is fair,
Not with these weak limbs is thy last race run;
Not all thy vision sets with this low sun;
Not all thy spirit swoons with this despair.

FROM POETRY

Look how thine own soul, throned where all is well,
Smiles to regard thy days disconsolate;
Yea; since herself she wove the worldly spell
Doomed thee for lofty gain to low estate,
Sown with thy fall a seed of glory fell;
Thy heaven is in thee, and thy will thy fate.

Inward! Ay, deeper far than love or scorn,
Deeper than bloom of virtue, stain of sin,
Rend thou the veil and pass alone within,
Stand naked there and feel thyself forlorn!
Nay! In what world then spirit wast thou born
Or to what world-soul art thou entered in?
Feel the self fade, feel the great life begin,
With love re-rising in the cosmic morn.
The inward ardour yearns to the inmost goal,
The endless goal is one with the endless way,
From every gulf the tides of being roll,
From every zenith burns the indwelling day,
And life in life has drowned thee, soul in soul,
And these are God, and thou thyself art they.

Frederick Myers (1843–1901)

The next two poems embrace a belief in reincarnation, the impression of having been here before.

A Creed

I held that when a person dies
His soul returns again to earth;
Arrayed in some new flesh-disguise,
Another mother gives him birth.
With sturdier limbs and brighter brain
The old soul takes the road again.

And as I wander on the roads
I shall be helped and healed and blessed;
Kind words shall cheer and be as goads
To urge to heights before unguessed.
My road shall be the road I made,
All that I gave shall be repaid.

THE SACRED QUEST

So shall I fight, so shall I tread,
In this long war beneath the stars;
So shall a glory wreathe my head,
So shall I faint and show the scars,
Until this case, this clogging mould,
Be smithied all to kingly gold.

John Masefield (1878–1967)

Sudden Light

I have been here before,
But when or how I cannot tell;
I know the grass beyond the door,
The sweet keen smell,
The sighing sound, the lights around the shore.

You have been mine before, –
How long ago I may not know:
But just when at that swallow's soar
Your neck turned so,
Some veil did fall, – I knew it all of yore.

Dante Gabriel Rossetti (1828–82)

The next poem is an imaginative treatment of the same theme.

The Trial by Existence

The light of heaven falls whole and white
And is not shattered into dyes,
The light forever is morning light;
The hills are verdured pasture-wise;
The angel hosts with freshness go,
And seek with laughter what to brave; –
And binding all is the hushed snow
Of the far-distant breaking wave.

And from a cliff-top is proclaimed
The gathering of the souls for birth,
The trial by existence named,
The obscuration upon earth.
And the slant spirits trooping by
In streams and cross – and counter-streams
Can but give ear to that sweet cry
For its suggestion of what dreams!

48

And the more loitering are turned
To view once more the sacrifice
Of those who for some good discerned
Will gladly give up paradise.
And a white shimmering concourse rolls
Toward the throne to witness there
The speeding of devoted souls
Which God makes his especial care.

And so the choice must be again,
But the last choice is still the same;
And the awe passes wonder then,
And a hush falls for all acclaim.
And God has taken a flower of gold
And broken it, and used therefrom
The mystic link to bind and hold
Spirit to matter till death come.

Robert Frost (1874–1963)

The last two poems selected – among the best known in the English language – express deep mystical insight.

The Hound of Heaven

I fled Him, down the nights and down the days;
I fled Him, down the arches of the years;
I fled Him, down the labyrinthine ways
Of my own mind; and in the mist of tears
I hid from Him, and under running laughter.
Up vistaed hopes I sped;
And shot, precipitated
Adown Titanic glooms of chasmed fears,
From those strong Feet that followed, followed after.
But with unhurrying chase,
And unperturbed pace,
Deliberate speed, majestic instancy,
They beat – and a Voice beat
More instant than the Feet –
'All things betray thee, who betrayest Me.'

Francis Thompson (1859–1907)

THE SACRED QUEST

Intimations of Immortality, from Recollections of Early Childhood

Our birth is but a sleep and a forgetting;
The soul that rises with us, our life's star,
Hath had elsewhere its setting
And cometh from afar.
Not in entire forgetfulness
And not in utter nakedness
But trailing clouds of glory do we come
From God who is our home.
Heaven lies about us in our infancy!
Shades of the prison house begin to close
Upon the growing boy;
But he beholds the light, and whence it flows
He sees it in his joy.

William Wordsworth (1770–1850)

The writer is fully aware that selecting poems – for any purpose – is a highly subjective undertaking, and for that very reason is somewhat hazardous! For in the matter of poetry, people's likes and dislikes can be both pronounced and unpredictable. But the poems quoted in this chapter do at least point to one very important conclusion: namely, that many of this country's best known poets were convinced of the existence of a reality which transcends the world of the five physical senses.

References

1. *The Human Situation*, W. Macneile Dixon, (Edward Arnold & Co., 1946. First published, 1937), p. 436
2. *Song and its Fountains*, A.E. (George Russell), (Macmillan & Co., 1932), p. 91
3. See *Man's Latent Powers*, Phoebe Payne, (Faber & Faber, 1938), p. 183

50

5: From The Paranormal

What mean these premonitions and apparitions, levitations and hauntings, these tales of far sight in time and in space, of pre-cognition and retro-cognition, of stigmata and faith cures, of crystal vision and alternating personalities, of dowsing and divining rods, of telepathy and hyperaesthesia, of hypnosis and suggestion – of which, it is said, there are some seven hundred explanatory theories – of monitions and intuitions like those of Socrates and Joan of Arc? They meet you everywhere, in every age, in every literature, in every quarter of the globe. Is it all crazy abracadabra, and is the whole world a madhouse? Do not let us talk of the credible and the incredible until we have looked further into these among many other things; from which, if well understood, a new vision of truth might arise.[1]

W. Macneile Dixon

We shall focus attention on three areas having far reaching implications for our particular field of enquiry: (A) Out-of-Body experiences. (B) Experiences indicating life after death. (C) Experiences suggestive of reincarnation. Many books and much attention have been devoted to (B), a considerable amount to (A), rather less to (C).

A. Out-of-Body Experiences

By analogy with a pianist and a piano, the mind corresponds to the pianist and the brain to the piano. If either pianist or piano is inadequate, so will be the music. If either mind or brain is inadequate, so will be the person.[2]

D. M. A. Leggett

51

An Out-of-Body experience, sometimes referred to as an 'ecsomatic experience', is 'one in which the objects of perception are apparently arranged in such a way that the observer seems to himself to be observing them from a point of view which is not coincident with his physical body'.[3] Such experiences may occur when the person concerned is what is normally referred to as unconscious due to an accident or anaesthetic, or is asleep, or is awake. The number of well authenticated cases must run into thousands;[4] the following examples are typical.

(i)   Person unconscious due to injury
An Officer – nearly killed in battle.[5]

In August 1944 his car received a direct hit from an anti-tank gun and he was thrown a distance of twenty feet.

'I was conscious of being two persons – one lying on the ground, on fire, waving my limbs about wildly and gibbering with fear – I was conscious of both making these sounds and at the same time hearing them as though coming from another person.

'The other "me" was floating up in the air, about twenty feet from the ground, from which position I could see not only my other self on the ground but also the hedge, the road and the burning car. I told myself, "It's no use gibbering: roll over and over to put the flames out." This my ground-body did. The flames went out and I suddenly became one person again.'

(ii)   Person unconscious due to accident
Mr Wheeler – nearly drowned.[6]

He said, 'While I was apparently dead, I never was so much alive in my life. But I was apart from my body. I could tell the persons around me everything that had happened when I was enabled to return. Being dead is delightful; of that I am sure. After I had been engulfed in the waters, I seemed to float away from my body, and soared above the waters of the lake. I looked down and could see my body. I watched the rescuers find it and place it on the bank. Then I floated back to it and became part of it. Up to the time of that experience I had been an agnostic, but I never since have had a shadow of doubt with regard to a spiritual state of existence.'

(iii)   Person unconscious due to anaesthetic
Mr Cole – nearly died.[7]

Mr Cole needed to have some teeth extracted. He dreamed that he was warned that he had heart trouble. However, a Dr Costello, who had called to see him on business, arranged to give the anaesthetic. Meanwhile, Mrs Cole also had a warning dream, though she did not tell her husband about it until after the operation. Mrs Cole dreamed that she saw her husband lying with a towel round his neck. On his cheek was a streak of blood which ran from the corner of the mouth and then at right angles up the cheek. She could not understand how the blood could run up the face. While Mrs Cole lay awake, Mr Cole came from the bathroom saying, 'I will have my teeth out after the holidays.' His wife connected this with her dream and told two members of Mr Cole's staff – this at a later date, but prior to the event itself.

Mr Cole was given the anaesthetic. His further account is as follows. 'The doctor pulled open my eye and said "He's gone!" but I could see his face and the lamp-shade, so I tried to say, "I'm not gone!" My words, however, were unheard and I let myself go. When I regained consciousness, I was outside my body, standing behind my own bed. My feeling of elation was indescribable. I was between the doctor and the dentist. They were talking about a house that was for sale and mentioned the price that was asked for it. I looked round the room and found that I was not alone, other people were there, the nearest to me being the (deceased) Italian lady of whom I had a sketch by the clairvoyant Ronald Bailey and a full description by Mrs Hester Dowden.

'The lady said, "We warned you about this, you know," and went on to say that there was some obscure heart trouble. Then I could see that the doctor had some doubt about my condition. I had stopped breathing. I heard him shout, "Breathe! breathe! Mr Cole!" Somehow, although I was outside my body, I managed to make my lungs start breathing again.

'The Italian lady said, "We are just keeping you alive by the vitality drawn from the doctor – we sent him to you." I could see the doctor's thoughts: he was afraid I might slip through his fingers. I went round to the other side of my body and saw that the dentist had removed all my teeth except seven in the lower jaw. The walls were curiously transparent: I could see into the passage, although the door was closed. Then I saw the table behind my body and, seeing the ether-bottle almost empty, thought "What a lot they have used." The Italian lady said "You must go back; you must make a fight for it. Never again have a general anaesthetic." So I turned away from the bright light which shone on my left and entered a gloomy tunnel. I fought my way back to a tiny light in the distance against a stream of shadows which passed all around me. When I got to the light, I found myself in bed.

'While I was still unconscious my wife had brought a member of the staff to see me, so that he could see that I was lying exactly as she had dreamed. The curious streak of blood, which she had seen in the dream had been caused by my cheek pressing against the pillow. The blood had trickled out of the corner of my mouth and then, when my head had flopped over to the opposite side, the dried blood ran up my cheek at an angle, as she had seen.

'I was too intent watching the little drama being played in the bedroom to make any observations about the psychic cord. I was certainly attached by something, otherwise I could not have made my body breathe when it had stopped.

'I checked up with the doctor next day, when he rang up to see how I was. He said that what I had heard of the conversation was correct. This was confirmed by the dentist. The latter also made a voluntary statement about the enormous amount of ether they had given me. The doctor was a big man, of immense vitality, and I am sure that the end might have been different had I gone to someone else.'

(iv)   Person asleep

Dr Paul Brunton at night in the Great Pyramid.[8]

He said, 'I gazed down upon the deserted body of flesh which was lying prone on the stone block. I noted a trail of faint silvery light projecting down from me, the new me, to the cataleptic creature who lay upon the block. Then I discovered that this mysterious psychical umbilical cord was contributing toward the illumination of the corner of the King's chamber where I hovered, showing up the wall-stones in a soft, moonbeam-like light.

'Yes, I had risen into space, disentangling my soul from its mortal skein. I experienced a sense of being etherealized, of intense lightness, in this duplicate body which I now inhabited. A single realization now overwhelmed me. "This is death. Now I know that I am a soul, that I can exist apart from the body." '

(v)   Person dozing

Rev. Dr Hepworth – in good health.[9]

Dr Hepworth said, 'I seemed to step out of my body, and stand beside it, looking down upon it. I felt as light as air, and thought, "This must be what St Paul calls the Spiritual Body." I moved away from my Physical Body towards the door, and to my surprise, I found that the door was no obstruction whatsoever: I simply passed through it. I knew that a cold wind was blowing, but I was not chilled. Then I stepped back into the room to get another glimpse of the body. "It is not dead," I said to myself, "only I have stepped out of it. I shall have to return to it by and by," and at that thought I shuddered. While I stood there, my dog Leo awoke. He approached my body in the usual way, with a wag of the tail, snuffed at my legs, and then appeared to be confused. Something was not as he expected to find it. He then deliberately snuffed at my legs a second time. Not satisfied, he sat on his haunches gazing into the face. I thought that perhaps his confusion arose from the fact that the eyes were closed. On ordinary occasions, when he wished to wake me from a doze, he put his paws on my knees, and gave a quick, sharp bark, as though to say, "Come, master, rouse yourself!" But this time he exhibited signs of terror and uttered a mournful howl. Then he apparently caught sight of me standing by the door. With a single leap, he reached my side, but turned instantly, took his place between me and the body, looked first at one and then at the other, and trembled in evident agony.'

(vi)   Person awake
From diary of Robert A. Monroe.[10]
   'R.W., a businesswoman whom I know quite well through long work association, has been away this week on her vacation up on the New Jersey coast. I do not know exactly where she is vacationing other than that. Nor did I inform her of any planned experiment, simply because I hadn't thought of it until today (Saturday). This afternoon, I lay down to renew experimentation, and decided I would make a strong effort to "visit" R.W. wherever she was.
   'There was the familiar sensation of movement through a light blue blurred area, when I was in what seemed to be a kitchen. R.W. was seated in a chair to the right. She had a glass in her hand. She was looking to my left, where two girls (about seventeen or eighteen, one blonde and one brunette) also were sitting, each with glasses in their hands, drinking something. The three of them were in conversation, but I could not hear what they were saying.
   'I first approached the two girls, directly in front of them, but I could not attract their attention. I then turned to R.W. and I asked if she knew I was there. "Oh yes, I know you are here," she replied (mentally, or with that super-conscious communication, as she was still in oral conversation with the two girls). I asked if she was sure that she would remember that I had been there. "I will remember, I'm sure I will,"

R.W. said, still in oral conversation simultaneously. I stated that I had to be sure she would remember, so I was going to pinch her. "Oh, you don't need to do that, I'll remember," R.W. said hastily. I said I had to be sure, so I reached over and tried to pinch her, gently, I thought. I pinched her in the side, just above the hips and below the rib cage. She let out a good loud "Ow", and I backed up, because I was somewhat surprised. I really hadn't expected to be able actually to pinch her. Satisfied that I had made some impression, at the least, I turned and left, thought of the physical, and was back almost immediately. R.W. will not be back until Monday, and then I can determine if I made the contact, or if it was another unidentifiable miss. Time of return, three thirty-five.

'Important aftermath: It is Tuesday after the Saturday of the experiment. R.W. returned to work yesterday, and I asked her what she had been doing Saturday afternoon between three and four. Knowing my reason for asking, she said she would have to think about it and let me know. Here is what she reported today: On Saturday between three and four was the only time there was not a crowd of people in the beach cottage where she was staying. For the first time, she was alone with her niece (dark-haired, about eighteen) and the niece's friend (about the same age, blonde). They were in the kitchen-dining area of the cottage from about three-fifteen to four, and she was having a drink, and the girls were having Cokes. They were doing nothing but sitting and talking.

'I asked R.W. if she remembered anything else, and she said no. I questioned her more closely, but she could not remember anything more. Finally, in impatience, I asked her if she remembered the pinch. A look of complete astonishment crossed her face. "Was that you?" She stared at me for a moment, then went into the privacy of my office, turned, and lifted the edge of her sweater where it joined her skirt on her left side. There were two brown and blue marks at exactly the spot where I had pinched her. "I was sitting

57

there, talking to the girls," R.W. said, "when all of a sudden I felt this terrible pinch. I must have jumped a foot. I thought my brother-in-law had come back and sneaked up behind me. I turned around, but there was no one there. I never had any idea it was you! It hurt!" '

From the preceding examples, and bearing in mind the existence of many others – the cases referred to in *Life after Life*[11] and *Reflections on Life after Life*[12] by Dr Raymond Moody for example – it seems clear that a significant number of ordinary people can function as self-conscious beings independently of their physical body. And if this is true for some people, is there any reason for thinking that it is not possible, at least potentially, for everyone? In addition to this fundamental conclusion there are a number of points which merit attention. Awareness of physical surroundings – all cases; the two 'me's, one of which can influence the other – cases (i) and (iii); sense of elation, except for apprehension about 'return' – cases (ii), (iii), and to some extent cases (iv) and (v); reference to psychic cord – cases (iii) and (iv); reference to duplicate body – case (iv); awareness of someone who had died – case (iii); awareness of other people's thoughts – cases (iii) and (vi). The precognitive dreams in case (iii), the dog's reactions in case (v), and the pinch in case (vi) are also of interest.

We shall conclude this section with three examples of a different kind.

(vii) From the diary of *The Boy Who Saw True*[13]
'You must pardon me for having disappeared so suddenly the other day, but I was called back to my body. As I gave you no reason to think otherwise, I expect you imagine I'm a dismembered spirit? But that's not exactly the case. To be explicit, I happen to be a so-called Anglo-Indian, and I am communicating with you while out of my body which is asleep, thousands of miles away from here. Our night is your day. If it were not, I shouldn't be able to come to you like this. I have learnt to do work on this plane in my astral body

while my physical body is asleep. Your young companion has the same power, and I often meet him over here. But neither he nor I remember it when we return to our bodies in the morning. Perhaps this seems strange to you, yet it's quite simple. Without special training, the astral body does not impress the physical brain with the memory of its experiences. Later on, the boy, who is a more advanced soul than I am, will probably acquire this faculty to some extent. But whether or no, both he and I may be said to lead double lives; there is our life on earth in the daytime, and our life over here at night. Of course if we try to communicate, as I am doing at present, with someone who can see – and there are not so many such as yet – there is always the possibility of being suddenly recalled to the physical body by a noise or something which wakes one up; and in that case, one vanishes in the disconcerting manner I vanished the other night, or rather day for you. However – there it is. And now after this lengthy explanation, what is it you were asking me?'

(viii)   From *The Silent Road* by W. Tudor Pole[14]
'I was living in a houseboat on the Nile. Apart from my Berberine servants, there was no one else on board. An occasion arose when a virulent fever laid me low and to such an extent that I could not make my servants understand that I wanted one of them to go down the river to Cairo to fetch a doctor.

'Whilst lying on my bunk, some seven days after the illness began, I heard a distinct knock on the cabin door. This was followed by the entry of a man who was evidently an Englishman of the professional class. Being in the height of summer, I remember wondering in a hazy way why my visitor was dressed in such unsuitable clothing for the climate, as he was wearing a frock coat and thick striped trousers. He carried a top hat in one hand and a stick and small black bag in the other.

'My visitor greeted me pleasantly and sat down on the side

of my bunk. I distinctly felt his weight upon the bed. Concluding that he must be a doctor, possibly sent out to see me from the Residency, I thanked him for calling, but added that he had come too late. He took no notice of this remark, but, after studying me closely, advised me to tell one of my servants to go to the Mosque at Cairo and to bring back from a herbalist's shop there a certain remedy for which he gave me the details. This herbal compound was to be infused in hot water and taken three times daily and I was to drink pure lemon juice but to take no solid food of any kind.

'I should have mentioned that on entering my cabin this visitor had placed his hat and stick on a small table behind which stood a mirror. During our conversation I happened to look at his hat and, to my surprise, found that I could see the mirror through it. Only then did it dawn on me that my visitor was not bodily present in the accepted meaning of the term. I asked him who he was and where he came from. He replied that he was a British doctor in regular practice. For some time past he said he had been in the habit of locking the door of his consulting room for an hour each evening, stilling his mind and, in prayer, asking that he might be sent wherever he could prove most useful. He added that he rarely remembered his experiences subsequently, although he always knew whether they had proved fruitful or not. After assuring me that I should soon be fit again (which forecast was fulfilled) he wished me well and went away.

'Still not being sure that my visitant had not been present in the flesh, I rang for my servant and asked whether he had escorted the doctor safely ashore. In surprise he assured me that no one had come on board throughout the day. I then sent my cook into Cairo, where he succeeded in finding the herbalist's shop and in bringing back the remedy that had been prescribed.

'Whether following the instructions related above resulted in my cure or whether this was brought about by the doctor's healing presence is a problem I have never solved, but the intervention described above undoubtedly saved my life.'

(ix) From *The Unfinished Autobiography* of Alice A. Bailey[15]

'It was a Sunday morning. This Sunday, for some reason, I had not gone to church. All the rest of the house-party had gone and there was no one in the house but myself and the servants. I was sitting in the drawing-room reading. The door opened and in walked a tall man dressed in European clothes (very well cut, I remember) but with a turban on his head. He came in and sat down beside me. I was so petrified at the sight of the turban that I could not make a sound or ask what he was doing there. Then he started to talk. He told me there was some work that it was planned that I could do in the world but that it would entail my changing my disposition very considerably; I would have to give up being such an unpleasant little girl and must try and get some measure of self-control. My future usefulness to him and to the world was dependent upon how I handled myself and the changes I could manage to make. He said that if I could achieve real self-control I could then be trusted and that I would travel all over the world and visit many countries, "doing your Master's work all the time". He emphasised that it all depended upon me.

'The interview was very brief. I said nothing but simply listened whilst he talked quite emphatically. Having said what he had come to say, he got up and walked out, after pausing at the door for a minute to give me a look which to this day I remember very distinctly.

'As the years went by I found that at seven years intervals (until I was thirty-five) I had indications of the supervision and interest of this individual. Then in 1915 I discovered who he was and that other people knew him. From then on the relationship has become closer and closer until today I can, at will, contact him.'

B. Survival

Grounds for an unusually intense fear of death are nowadays not far to seek: they are obvious enough, the more so as all life that is senselessly wasted and misdirected means death too. This may account for the unnatural intensification of the fear of death in our time, when life has lost its deeper meaning for so many people, forcing them to exchange the life-preserving rhythm of the aeons for the dread ticking of the clock.[16]

C. G. Jung

Do not seek death. Death will find you. But seek the road which makes death a fulfilment . . . In the last analysis, it is our conception of death which decides our answers to all the questions that life puts to us. That is why it requires its proper place and time – if need be with right of precedence. Hence, too, the necessity of preparing for it.[17]

Dag Hammarskjöld

The literature about life after death is vast in quantity and varied in quality. The subject has been surrounded with so much emotion and prejudice that it is not easy to consider the problem with emotional dispassion and intellectual honesty. Whether human life continues after death, and if it does what its nature may be, has troubled mankind since the dawn of history. The fact that there is no generally accepted answer after all this time indicates that the answer is unlikely to be simple. Is this, perchance, the reason why great religious teachers such as the Buddha and Jesus appear to have said so little about life after death? They knew that most of the ordinary men and women of their time would be quite unable to grasp the difficult concepts involved and that anything which they might say would be hopelessly misunderstood. What they taught to their disciples we do not know.

The main sources of evidence include (a) apparitions often at or near the moment of death; (b) automatic writing;

(c) mediums in trance; (d) sensitives, not in trance. In addition there is evidence or testimony which does not fall neatly into any of the above categories. Unfortunately the subject lends itself to deliberate fraud, for example materialisation in a darkened room, or, what is much more common, unconscious deception, for example attributing information picked up telepathically from those present to a discarnate communicator. This is *not* intended to imply that there is no such thing as materialisation or that information never comes from a discarnate source; merely that all evidence or testimony relating to such matters has to be examined with very great care. There are a number of points to be borne in mind.

First, because certain mediums and investigators have been shown, on occasion, to be guilty of deliberate fraud or unconscious deception, this is no reason for taking the view that all mediums and investigators are either frauds or deceivers. Such an attitude is no more logical than saying that because some witnesses in a court of law don't tell the truth, therefore none do. To be on one's guard is one thing; to adopt an *a priori* attitude of total disbelief is another.

Second, because of the unknown limits to the conceptual ability of the human brain in relation to extra sensory perception (ESP), it may well prove impossible to find a case that proves survival once and for all.

Third is the importance of cumulative evidence. Mathematically it can be shown that if five unreliable people, whose degree of unreliability is such that each one only tells the truth one time in five, *independently* assert that something happened, the probability is that it did indeed happen. The application of this to the matter under discussion is clear. If a large number of cases, each one of which is considered suspect on *a priori* grounds, all point in a particular direction, the probability that the direction is right may be high.

Fourth is the principle known as Occam's Razor.[18] This suggests that when confronted by the need to choose from a number of different hypotheses, the most expedient choice, other things being equal, is to select the simplest.

There now follow five illustrative cases which have been selected from a large number. Cases (i) to (iii) are typical; cases (iv) and (v) are not.

(i)   Apparition – at or near moment of death[20]
The Jennie Case.[19]

In a neighbouring city were two little girls, Jennie and Edith, one about eight years of age, and the other a little older. They were school-mates and intimate friends. Both were taken ill of diphtheria. On Wednesday, Jennie died. Then the parents of Edith, and her physician as well, took particular pains to keep from her the fact that her little playmate was gone. They feared the effect of the knowledge on her own condition.

She (Edith) died at half-past six on Saturday evening. She had roused and bidden her friends good-bye, and was talking of dying persons and seemed to have no fear. She appeared to see one and another of the friends she knew were dead. But now, suddenly and with every appearance of surprise, she turned to her father and exclaimed, 'Why, papa, I am going to take Jennie with me!' And immediately she reached out her arms as if in welcome, and said, 'O, Jennie, I'm so glad you are here.'

(ii)   Automatic Writing
Mrs Willett's repentance.[21]

Between 1957 and 1960, Geraldine Cummins, through the medium of automatic writing, ostensibly acted as a means of communication for Mrs Coombe Tennant who had died in 1956 and who was known to the world of psychic investigators during her life time as Mrs Willett. What follows is an extract from a communication addressed to her second son Alexander.

'My dear, dear Alexander,
     It is my urgent need to write to you on a private matter that concerns us two. I have a humiliating confession to

make and must cast away all pride. I have been a witness of the film of memory, the record of my life. There are, as you may know, underground chambers of the mind, certain of them might be likened to foul festering dungeons. I have very recently had a dismaying revelation of one of them. I feel I must share it with you or in future I shall have no peace of mind.'

She then very carefully describes her capricious and baffled emotional vanity which built up a psychological barrier between them and goes on to say: 'Mine has been the initial offence all along. If at any time you have felt a barrier between us I created it not you. For the sake of my peace of mind I beg of you to forgive my grievous fault.'

As Paul Beard observes 'It is hard to suppose that this heartfelt apology came from the automatist's perception of the emotional needs of the son whom she had not met.'

A penetrating analysis and appraisal of a whole series of communications is given by Professor C. D. Broad in his foreword to *Swan on a Black Sea*.

(iii)   Medium – in trance
The Case of the Shark.[22]

'The Australian banker, Hugh Junor Browne . . . had the misfortune to lose his two sons during a cruise they were making in their yacht . . . The parents were very anxious when their sons did not return, and applied for information to the . . . medium . . . George Sprigg . . . One of Mr Browne's sons manifested through the medium's mouth, furnishing . . . details of the drama, among them the tragic particular that his brother's body had been mutilated of an arm by a shark. This was confirmed in an extraordinary manner, for a shark was caught in whose stomach Hugh's arm was found, together with a piece of his waistcoat, his watch and a few coins. The watch had stopped at nine o'clock, the hour indicated by the medium as that when the shipwreck took place.'

It is likely that this is about as near to a black and white case as it is possible to get in that no living person witnessed the events described.

(iv) Sensitive – not in trance
A personal experience of the writer.

In July 1961 I was one of about 120 people attending a weekend conference. After lunch on the Saturday I was talking with two ladies, Miss F. and Mrs H. We were seated round a small table in one corner of the large lecture hall which was empty except for the three of us. Miss F. I knew fairly well; Mrs H. I had only met on two or three previous occasions.

I was talking and in the middle of a sentence, when Mrs H. lent over and said: 'I am sorry to interrupt you but there is a presence – just behind you. It is your mother.' For two or three minutes Mrs H. then repeated to me what she 'heard' my 'mother' say. (Hearing in a case like this is not through the physical ear; the process corresponds to what you hear when you rehearse to yourself a speech or conversation but do not speak.) What was said was what I should have expected my mother to say on such an occasion. The bond between us was very strong, and much of what she said was intimate. The background to many of her remarks could not possibly have been known to Miss F. or Mrs H. by normal means, and one or two matters touched on could only have had meaning for myself. But to begin with nothing was said which could not have been picked up from my mind telepathically by Mrs H., and put together unconsciously to produce what my 'mother' said. Later, however, two matters were mentioned for which a telepathic explanation seems inadequate. Two developments were predicted which at the time seemed most improbable. Within three or four years both developments had taken place.

I would estimate that the whole experience, which took me completely by surprise, lasted for a little under five minutes. Throughout I said nothing. There are times in life when one is moved to silence; this for me was one of them.

As a matter of fact my mother had died some eighteen months before, in December 1959. During the preceding year or two she and I both knew that she had not long to live, and we had talked freely about death and possible after death conditions. I had told her that I did not intend trying to 'get in touch' through a medium. But we had agreed that if she found it possible to give me some indication of her continued existence she would do so.

Miss F. and Mrs H. both said that I had never mentioned my mother to them – there was no reason why I should – so that they did not know at the time whether or not she was alive.

Miss F. said that she, too, was aware of a presence, but not being clairaudient did not 'hear' what my 'mother' said.

(v) A very special apparition
Described by the Rev. Dr Leslie D. Weatherhead.[23]

'Let me tell you a story for which I can personally vouch. A minister was sitting alone in his study one stormy night, when he heard the bell ring. Going to the door, he found standing there a young woman whom he knew fairly well. She was from a village some five miles away. This village was in an adjoining circuit from which the minister in question had moved some sixteen months before. "Good evening," she cried. "I expect you have forgotten me, but I have come on a very urgent errand. My father is dying. He never attended church much, but once or twice when you were in the circuit we persuaded him to hear you preach. I *do* wish you would come and pray with him before he passes away." "I will come at once," replied the minister. Putting on his coat and hat, and taking an umbrella from the stand, he set off in the pouring rain on a five-mile walk, accompanied by the young woman.

'On his arrival at the house, the wife welcomed him warmly. "Oh, how good of you to come!" she said. "But how did you know that my husband was passing away?" "Your daughter came for me," he replied, with some surprise at the question.

'It was the woman's turn to be surprised now. "Come upstairs at once," she said, "and we will talk afterwards."

'The minister went to the bedside of the dying man, spoke to him, and prayed with him, and shortly afterwards the end came. Turning to the woman, who was now a widow, he asked where the daughter was, for he had not seen her again since they entered the house. The woman replied, "I was surprised when you came to the door this evening, and I asked you who told you that my husband was dying. You said my daughter called, and that you came out together. You have not heard, then, that my daughter died a year ago?"

'Now the minister was astounded indeed. "Dead!" he exclaimed. "She came to my door, rang the bell, and walked out here with me. But there," he said, "I think I can prove that. As we came along together the road was up in one place, and a watchman and another man were sitting in a hut in front of a fire. They saw us go by. I'll speak to them on my way home."

'He set off on his return journey, and found the two men still sitting in front of the fire. "You saw me go by an hour or so ago, didn't you?" he said to the men. "Was I alone?" "Yes, sir," one of them replied, "and you were talking away to yourself as hard as you could!" '

Dr Weatherhead's concluding comment was 'At the time, of course, just as at Emmaus, there was nothing strange about this "appearance".'

Having regard to the existence of so much evidence, of which what has been described is only a tiny though representative sample, the writer concludes that the essential part of a person's personality does indeed survive physical death and that this has been established 'beyond reasonable doubt'.[24]

If the assumption is now made that there is some kind of existence after physical death and the question is asked as to its nature, the following cases, all taken from Dr Crookall's book *The Supreme Adventure*,[25] are relevant. They are ostensible communications from people who have died.

FROM THE PARANORMAL

(a)   What impressed me most, after a period of rest, was the reality of all things. My body seemed as tangible as before the change . . . my senses were more acute. I saw running brooks, lakes, trees, grass and flowers. I took long deep breaths of wonderfully vitalising air.

(b)   There seemed to be a period of unconsciousness. Then I awoke . . . Death really is just a sleep and an awakening.

(c)   I seemed to pass into a peaceful sleep . . . I hear now that I must have slept for three or four days . . . When I woke completely I felt so refreshed . . . I knew I was not on earth, not only because of the long lost people around me again, but because of the brilliancy of the atmosphere.

Also:

(d)   The Day of Judgment does not take place on our immediate arrival here. The word 'day' is incorrect, for the trial is not limited to twenty-four hours. It is not possible to talk of it in terms of earth-time. But there is a special period when we enter the Gallery of Memory and the pictures of our earth-life pass before us. Then our Spirit is our Judge. We face this time when we are fit for it.

(e)   My past deeds crowded before me . . . Little or great, nothing was forgotten. At last an inspiration seemed to seize me and I prayed. I had not done so for years, but now I prayed and, as I did so, the chaos began to sort itself out. It took chronological order . . . Among the visions I saw some which came as a relief to my tired soul – little acts of kindness which I had long forgotten . . . So I found my location.

(f)   The Judgment consists in being able to see ourselves as we are, and by no stretch of imagination being able to avoid seeing it. It is a Judgment of God on us through our Higher Selves. On earth, even the best are subconsciously avoiding things, or trying to think things are slightly other than they are . . . No other person could be so just a Judge as we ourselves can be when facing the truth. For many it is a terrible hour . . . Directly one has realised how, where and why one was wrong, there is an instinctive feeling that one must work it out. And

69

this way of recovery is in helping others who have exactly similar limitations, difficulties or vices.

The preceding cases indicate two things. Cases (a) to (c) emphasise the apparent objectivity of conditions immediately after 'waking up'. Cases (d) and (f) refer to an experience of the greatest possible significance, the 'judgment', which nobody, it seems, can avoid.

We have now reached a point at which the reader would be well advised to consult one or two books, for example *The Supreme Adventure* by Dr Crookall,[25] *Survival of Death*[22] and *Living On* by Paul Beard,[26] and *Survival* by David Lorimer.[27] *Survival of Death* shows with exemplary thoroughness how easy it is to jump to a conclusion, for example of survival, which is not warranted after a sufficiently careful study of the evidence. The other books indicate the amount and nature of the available evidence.

We shall conclude this section by referring to evidence of a different kind, to accounts of what seem to be a relationship extending over a considerable period of time between someone who is living and someone who is dead. In these cases there is no substitute for reading some of the books which describe this kind of evidence. Three such books are *A Woman of Spirit* by Doris Collins,[28] *The Country Beyond* by Jane Sherwood,[29] and *The Testimony of Light* by Helen Greaves.[30] After perusing any or all of these books the reader will have to make up his mind about what weight to attach to what is described. In particular, does the totality of what is said sound authentic and ring true, or doesn't it?

C. Reincarnation

How many modes of existence are there? I cannot tell you, but I should imagine them to be very numerous. And what kind of immortality is at all conceivable? Of all doctrines of a future life palingenesis or rebirth, which carries with it the idea of pre-existence, is by far the most ancient and most widely held, 'the only system to which', said Hume, 'philosophy can hearken'. 'The soul is eternal and migratory, say the Egyptians,' reports Laertius. In its existence birth and death are events. And though this doctrine has for European thought a strangeness, it is in fact the most natural and easily imagined, since what has been can be again. This belief, taught by Pythagoras, to which Plato and Plotinus were attached, has been held by Christian fathers as well as by many philosophers since the dawn of civilisation. It 'has made the tour of the world', and seems, indeed, to be in accordance with nature's own favourite way of thought, of which she so insistently reminds us, in her rhythms and recurrences, her cycles and revolving seasons. 'It presents itself,' wrote Schopenhauer, 'as the natural conviction of man whenever he reflects at all in an unprejudiced manner.'[31]

W. Macneile Dixon

Knowledge of previous incarnations becomes available when the power to see thought-images is acquired.[32]

Aphorisms of Patanjali

The rest of this chapter is in three sub-sections. The first sub-section describes experiences suggestive of a previous life; the second refers to some general considerations about the concept of reincarnation and looks at the attitude to it in early Christianity; the third comments on one of the arguments most frequently advanced against a reincarnationist hypothesis.

Sub-Section 1.   Ostensible Memories

We shall begin with four cases, chosen from a significant number. In the first two cases the interval between lives is only a few years; in the other two the interval is much longer.

(i)   Case of Alexandrina Samona
From *The Problem of Rebirth* by Hon. Ralph Shirley.[33]

'In 1910 Alexandrina Samona, five-year-old daughter of Dr and Mrs Samona, died of meningitis. Three days later Mrs Samona had a dream in which Alexandrina seemed to appear to her and say "Mother, don't cry any more; I have not left you for good; I will come back again. Little, like this." In the dream the child gestured with her hands to indicate a small baby. Communications along the same line were obtained by the Samonas in séances during which the deceased Alexandrina purported to foretell her return as a new baby together with a baby sister. Owing to Mrs Samona's physical condition the successful birth of one baby, let alone of twins, seemed highly improbable. However, within a year Mrs Samona did give birth to twin girls, one of whom bore an extraordinary physical resemblance to the first Alexandrina and was given the same name. Alexandrina II resembled Alexandrina I not only in appearance but also in temperament and in all sorts of likes and dislikes.

'When Alexandrina II was eight, her parents told her they planned to take her to visit Monreale and see the sights there. At this Alexandrina II interjected: "But, Mother, I know Monreale, I have seen it already." Mrs Samona told the child she had never been to Monreale, but the child replied: "Oh, yes, I went there. Do you not recollect that there was a great church with a very large statue of a man with his arms held open, on the roof? And don't you remember that we went there with a lady who had horns and that we met with some little red priests in the town?" At this Mrs Samona recollected that the last time she went to Monreale she had gone there with Alexandrina I some months before her death. They had taken with them a lady friend who had come to Palermo for a medical consultation as she suffered from disfiguring excrescences on her forehead. As they were going into the church the Samona's party had met a group of young Greek priests with robes decorated with red ornamentation. As the child apparently recalled incidents and not merely scenes at Monreale, she could not have derived the statements from a picture or photograph of the place. Mrs Samona only with difficulty recalled the episode when Alexandrina II mentioned it, so it is unlikely that she had previously told Alexandrina II about it. It is not, however, impossible for her to have done this and subsequently forgotten the episode and its narration to Alexandrina II.'

(ii)   Case of Shanti Devi[34]
From *Evidence for Survival from Claimed Memories of Former Incarnations* by Professor Ian Stevenson.

'In October 1925 Lugdi Devi died in childbirth in the hospital of the city of Muttra. She was 23. In December 1926 Shanti Devi was born in Delhi, about 80 miles away. There was never any connection between the two girls or their families. Yet when she was four years old Shanti suddenly began to live her life as Lugdi would have done. Lugdi was the wife of a Brahmin, the highest caste of Hindu. She was a devout girl who followed all the precepts of her religion and caste. Even her food was prepared in the manner traditional with Brahmins. Shanti had none of this caste background but one day, when her mother brought food to her she said she didn't like it. She asked for Brahmin food. Shanti described to her parents the clothes she used to wear. And her description tallied exactly with the traditional Brahmin dress. She began to speak in the dialect peculiar to the Muttra district. When her parents asked her how she came to know it she said simply: "I spent my prevous life there and it comes to me naturally." She stated that she had been born in 1902, and had married a cloth merchant named Kedar Chaubey. She said that she had given birth to a son and she had died ten days later.

'As Shanti continued to make such statements, her family finally wrote when she was nine years old to see if such a person as her claimed husband actually existed in Muttra. This person answered the letter and confirmed the girl's statements. He then sent a relative to the girl's home and afterwards came unannounced himself. She immediately identified both of these persons. The following year (1935), after it had been established that the girl had never left

73

Delhi, a committee was appointed to witness a visit by the girl to Muttra with a view to noting her recognition of people and places. At the railway station of Muttra she was put in a carriage the driver of which was instructed to follow her directions. These led to the district and the house of Kedar Chaubey which she recognised even though it had been repainted a different colour. In the area of the house an old Brahmin appeared and she identified him correctly as Kedar Chaubey's father. She also went to the house of her (claimed) previous parents who she correctly identified out of a crowd of more than fifty persons and correctly called them by name. Shanti claimed to have hidden some money in another house, the one which was the home of Kedar Chaubey's family. In this house she pointed to a corner of one of the rooms as the place where she had buried the money. When a hole was dug, the witnesses came to an arrangement for keeping valuables but found it empty. Shanti insisted she had left money there and eventually Kedar Chaubey acknowledged that he had found and removed the money after his wife's death.'

(iii)   Case of A.E. and P.G.B.
P.G.B. was a close friend of the late H. K. Challoner, someone I knew well. What follows is an extract from a letter she sent me.
'The meeting was between A.E. and P.G.B. at a party in Dublin. They had never set eyes on each other before and directly they were introduced, A.E. said, "We have met before"; P.G.B. replied, "Yes – I know." A.E. then suggested they should each go away and write down any memories they might have of the life in which they had been associated. When they compared notes, the description of an episode in Spain at the time of the Inquisition tallied in every detail. They were holding an occult meeting in a room when the soldiers burst in, and in the ensuing fight they were both killed.'

(iv)   Case of Mrs Weisz-Roos[35]
From *The Evidence for Survival from Claimed Memories of Former Incarnation* by Professor Ian Stevenson.

'A Dutch portrait painter named Henriette Roos married a man called Weisz whom she subsequently divorced. Although it is the custom in Holland for women to resume their maiden names after a divorce, Mrs Weisz for an unaccountable reason liked her married name and did not want to give it up. When her mother reproached her with not resuming her maiden name, she replied: "I don't know, it is a strange feeling, I can't explain, that name somehow suits me. I feel one with it, it is more me than my own name, Roos. Each time I call myself that way I have the feeling I'm talking about someone else." So she decided to call herself Mrs Weisz-Roos.

'Some time after her divorce she was in Paris working hard to support herself by her painting. One evening she went to bed extremely fatigued hoping to benefit from a good sleep. She then heard a voice say, or was impressed by the thought: "Don't be so lazy, get up and work." After further importuning which she at first resisted, she did get up and went to her easel. She was impressed to paint in the dark and did so with feverish haste and hardly knowing what she was doing. After a time she felt better, naturally sleepy and returned to bed and to sleep. Upon awakening the next morning, she discovered that she had painted a beautiful little portrait of a young woman.

'Puzzled by this experience, she described it to a friend who persuaded her to consult a sensitive who practised psychometry. Mrs Weisz-Roos took her portrait to the sensitive and without saying anything to her, placed it on a table from which the sensitive picked it up. The sensitive went into a trance and after a time said, "I see very large golden letters. A name is spelled to me – G O Y A; now he speaks to me. He says: He was a great Spanish painter. He had to fly from his country from his enemies and it was you who received him in your home in a big southern city in

France – until the end of his life. He still is so thankful for this that he wants to guide you – but he is not satisfied, you resist too much, you are too much tied up in your academic education – you never relax and let him guide you, you make it very difficult for him – he therefore made you paint in the dark so you couldn't see what you were doing."

'At the time of this communication, Mrs Weisz-Roos had never read anything about Goya. However, that same evening, she went to a home where her host owned a copy of a life of Goya. She borrowed this and was astonished to find in it an account of Leocadia Weisz, in whose home Goya had lived during his exile from Spain at the end of his life.'

A most thorough and penetrating analysis of cases similar to those just described has been undertaken by Professor Ian Stevenson and is given in his books, *Twenty Cases Suggestive of Reincarnation*;[36] and *Cases of the Reincarnation Type*, Vol. 1, *Ten Cases in India*, Vol. 11, *Ten Cases in Sri Lanka*.[37] To summarise such books is impossible. To appreciate the care and scholarship which he has devoted to examining the various cases the books must be studied.

Reference will now be made to evidence of a rather different kind; to the 'readings' of Edgar Cayce, and to two books – *Second Time Round* by E. W. Ryall,[38] and *The Wheel of Rebirth* by H. K. Challenor.[39]

Edgar Cayce was born in Kentucky, U.S.A. in 1877 of uneducated farming parents, and he too had little formal education. Life on the farm did not appeal, so he migrated to town where he worked first as clerk in a bookshop and then as an insurance salesman. When 21, he contracted laryngitis and lost his voice – not just temporarily. Shortly afterwards he met a hypnotist, named Hart, who offered to attempt a cure by the use of hypnotism. The attempt proved tantalising rather than successful in that when under hypnosis Cayce responded to Hart's suggestion and talked in a normal voice, but after awakening Cayce still could not speak. It was suggested by Layne, another hypnotist, that

Cayce should describe the nature of his ailment when under hypnosis. This he did, and as a result of his diagnosis and the ensuing treatment Cayce recovered the use of his voice. This was the start. From now on Cayce, under hypnosis, gave information, help and guidance, to innumerable people of every sort and kind. After many years of humanitarian activity, it occurred to Arthur Lammers, a well-to-do printer of Dayton, that Cayce under hypnosis might be able to provide information, not just about a person's physical or psychological condition, but about more general matters. This extended the information provided by Cayce when under hypnosis, and included references to a person's previous incarnations, and to how what he or she had been or had done then, was responsible for what he or she was, or was doing, now. By the time of his death Cayce had given some 2500 of these 'life readings' as they were called. To appraise this evidence, it must be studied, and *Many Mansions* and *The World Within* by Gina Cerminara[40] afford a good starting point. Further evidence of a comparable kind is described in *Many Lifetimes* by Joan Grant and Denys Kelsey,[41] and *Life before Life* by Helen Wambach.[42]

An unusual case was described by Maurice Blake, a hypnotist, in an article published in the *East Anglia Monthly* of August 1978. What follows is an extract.

> Mrs Margaret Baker had volunteered to assist me at a demonstration given to a meeting of the Norwich Astrological Society, about twenty of whose members were present. I rapidly induced a deep trance in Margaret and asked her to relive and describe any one of her former lives, using her subconscious memory (cf. the reference to 'man's unconscious mind', in chapter 7, page 108, line 4). Within a couple of minutes, Margaret began a dialogue with me in which, speaking in a male voice and using a gipsy dialect with many Romany words completely unknown to either of us, she recounted her life as a gipsy horse dealer, Tyso No Name Boswell.
> In forty minutes of fascinating dialogue, Tyso revealed a typical gipsy mentality, often suspicious and secretive,

sometimes aggressive, humorous and alert. Neither Margaret nor I had the slightest knowledge of Romany language, life or customs, and on being restored to her normal state of consciousness she did not know a word she had said until the tape recording was played back.

When told that his last day had come and his life was drawing to a close, Tyso found himself attending Horncastle Fair, and camping at the gipsy's camp site at Tetford. The weather, he said was 'dreadful'. Tyso and his inseparable companion Ted Heron crossed a field near the church and sheltered in a hovel. He was then silent for a minute.

M.   Are you sheltering? Did you reach the shelter and get there?

T.   Oh, yeah (grimly), we reached it alright.

M.   And then . . .?

T.   Reckon it must 'a bin the Wrath of God!

M.   What happened?

T.   The lightning. Got us both, yer know.

He went on to predict that he and Ted would be buried in the churchyard at Tetford and that a stone would be set up by his son. He gave the date clearly and precisely: August 5th, 1831.

Within a week the Vicar of St Mary's, Tetford, the Rev. P. Fluck, wrote confirming the entry in the Parish Register of the burial of two 'vagrants', Tyso Boswell and Edward Hearin on August 7th, 1831. The inscription on the gravestone reads:

> In Memory of Tyso Boswell, who was
> slain by lightening, Aug 5th, 1830, aged 56.
> Edward Hearin, who was slain by light-
> ening, Aug 5th, 1830, aged 70.

The monumental mason made a monumental error in his inscription, burying them in a common grave a year before they died. He evidently tried to correct his error, without much success. The gravestone is clearly legible despite its 147 years of exposure.

In a letter to the writer Mr Blake says: 'Nobody concerned with this case knew of the obscure village of Tetford before the session', and 'The Vicar asserted that no one had asked to see the Parish Register for at least five years'.

Whether this case should be regarded as evidence for

reincarnation or possession by a being who is earthbound is open to question. But it certainly indicates one or the other.

Second Time Round by Ryall is an ostensible case of far memory. In considerable detail the author describes his life as John Fletcher, a yeoman farmer who was born in Somerset in 1645 and who died at the battle of Sedgemoor in 1685. Professor Ian Stevenson, who has examined the case with care, states in his introduction to the book: 'This brings me to say therefore, that, as of now, I believe it best interpreted as an instance of reincarnation. In other words, I think it most probable that he has memories of a real previous life and that he is indeed John Fletcher reborn, as he believes himself to be.'

The Wheel of Rebirth is an autobiography, but of an unusual kind in that it covers seven lives. With the aid of a Teacher the author, through dreams, automatic writing and in other ways, was able to recall and to relive vital episodes in previous lives. Each chapter in the book is devoted to a life, and at the end of each chapter are the Teacher's comments on the life in question. Herein lies the value of the book. About the end of an utterly disastrous life in Greece, the Teacher comments: 'You did not die by your own hand as you imagined; you had done that in several previous incarnations and the futility of such an action had remained part of your mental equipment for all time. On the contrary, those years although apparently so horrible and degraded were the most fruitful of all. For, admitting failure, you sought at last to understand *where* you had failed. You no longer made excuses, you no longer blamed everything but yourself. Free at last of self-deception, you repented; but it was the real repentance. Not based on fear or hope of reward as in Egypt, this was inspired by love and an increased understanding of the Law. You did not alter your way of living – it was too late; but driven down among the dregs of humanity, you developed understanding, love, and sympathy for your fellow sufferers. Although you knew it not, this experience was a great act of spiritual growth.' The aims and values of a Teacher – one who is pre-eminently concerned with the spiritual development of individuals and of the race – tend to be somewhat different from the aims and values of the contemporary world! Like the other books already referred to, this, too, has to be read to be appreciated.

Reference will now be made to what is, perhaps, the most significant evidence of all – the experiences of a group of people described by Dr Arthur Guirdham in *The Cathars and Reincarnation*[43] and *We are One Another.*[44]

The Cathars and Reincarnation is the factual record of a woman who through dreams and impressions in waking consciousness ostensibly remembers her life as a Cathar in the 13th century. What is striking is the extent to which her recollections have been confirmed by subsequent research by Dr Guirdham. *We are One Another* describes how a group of Cathars who had lived and suffered together in the 13th century met again in this century in a limited area in the West of England. Independently of each other these people tuned in to the same tragic events in the Languedoc in the years 1242–44. By extensive research Dr Guirdham has discovered the mediaeval names and roles of seven out of the eight people principally concerned. The cross linking between different members of the group is so extensive that super ESP is, on the face of it, not a credible alternative to some sort of reincarnationist hypothesis.

It is also interesting to note that the three books referred to on p. 70 at the end of Section B, all accept the idea of reincarnation. What follows are extracts from *The Country Beyond* and *The Testimony of Light*.

> But it is rather like coming to the end of a long tunnel and suddenly finding an extensive view opening out ahead. For now, beyond birth the great perspective of past lives begins to open up. They are distant and they have not to be lived out in detail as one's latest life has been but they begin to come clearly into consciousness for acceptance by the ego and for inclusion in the sum total of experiences which have built up the personality.[45]

You ask about precognition and whether it is a fact that the future is foreseeable. As far as my experience goes, and as far as this new extension of my consciousness reveals facts about earth-life time, I am becoming increasingly aware of a Pattern and a Plan. The Blueprint of one's efforts, one's successes and failures on all the planes: physical, material, emotional, mental and spiritual does indicate that a definite line of advance is voluntarily accepted by the soul before incarnation.

No doubt when I am more proficient in the study of individual lives and their results, together with the life courses of nations and their results, good or apparently not good, which have been set in motion through the Law of Cause and Effect, I shall be better able to appreciate how the Divine Pattern of individual growth and group growth is linking up from life to life and from age to age. It is only logical to assume that we take up, as it were, where we left off in a previous trial of strength and weakness. This presupposes a chain of lives, of experiences, of reincarnation in its little understood form. But I am more than convinced, as I observe stories of effort and success and failure, that the soul needs to 'project' some part of itself back into the denser environment of earth in repeated attempts to master the trials and stresses of those vibrations. But which part of itself, and whether it is always the same part, is still a mystery, and must remain so until we have advanced much in wisdom and insight.[46]

In concluding this section it seems appropriate to mention three reference books: *Reincarnation in World Thought*, [47] *Reincarnation – an East–West Anthology*, [48] and *Reincarnation: The Phoenix Fire Mystery*,[49] by Joseph Head and S. L. Cranston. To those unfamiliar with the idea of reincarnation, it may come as a surprise to realise from a quick glance at these three books how many eminent people have viewed the idea sympathetically.

Sub-Section 2.   Some General Considerations

(i)   In every civilisation worthy of the name, the concept and administration of justice have played an important part. Ideas as to what constituted justice have varied widely, but the deliberate flouting, whether by individuals or by governments, of whatever was held at the time to be justice has invariably provoked strong and widespread protest.

With this in mind what are we to make of a world in which human beings are born with such staggeringly different talents and opportunities: a mentally defective child born into an unhappy home in an industrial slum at one end, and a superbly gifted child born into a happy home in pleasant surroundings at the other. Just? No. But what a strange situation: mankind dedicated to justice so far as material things are concerned, yet faced by an almost total lack of justice in relation to the non-material side of life. A lack, moreover, about which man can do very little.

When confronted by an anomaly, it is often helpful to go back to first principles and examine the underlying definitions and assumptions. In the case of justice the question immediately arises, justice to what end? The significance of this question can be seen from two, among many, possible answers. One, 'To ensure man's material well-being'; the other, 'To foster man's spiritual development.' When thought through, the consequences which flow from these two answers may be, and indeed will be, very different. What does this imply?

If a human life is regarded as starting at birth, the problem of justice, however defined, remains acute and on the face of it insoluble. If a human life is regarded as one of a series, and as providing an opportunity to learn a particular lesson from a particular experience, with the long term aim of approaching ever more nearly to spiritual maturity, the problem of justice becomes less acute, and may indeed be susceptible to a measure of resolution. It may be significant that we all know people, albeit not very many, who seem strangely mature and able to draw on a store of wisdom which their existing life could scarcely have provided.

(ii) Having regard to the crucial position which the concepts of karma and reincarnation occupy in two of the world's great religions – Buddhism and Hinduism – it seems surprising that so little attention has been paid to these concepts by adherents to the Christian tradition. The surprise increases when note is taken of the consideration which was given to the concept by a number of the early Church Fathers. Origen (185–254), one of the most celebrated, states:

> The soul, which is immaterial and invisible in its nature, exists in no material place without having a body suited to the nature of that place; accordingly it at one time puts off one body, which was necessary before but which is no longer adequate for its changed state, and it exchanges it for a second.
>
> The soul has neither beginning nor end . . . Every soul comes into this world strengthened by the victories or weakened by the defeats of its previous life. Its place in this world as a vessel appointed to honour or dishonour is determined by its previous merits or demerits.[50]

That the idea of reincarnation was not unfamiliar at the time of Jesus seems clear from the following quotations.

> Behold, I will send you Elijah the prophet before the coming of the great and dreadful day of the Lord.
>
> Malachi 4:5

> And Jesus said. For all the prophets and the law prophesied until John. And if ye will receive *it*, this is Elias, which was for to come. He that hath ears to hear, let him hear.
>
> Matthew 11:13, 14

> And Jesus answered and said unto them, Elias truly shall first come, and restore all things. But I say unto you, That Elias is come already, and they knew him not, but have done unto him whatsoever they listed. Likewise shall also the Son of man suffer of them. Then the disciples understood that he spake unto them of John the Baptist.
>
> Matthew 17:11–13

That the idea of pre-existence was current at the time of Jesus is shown by the question asked by his disciples: 'Master, who did sin, this man or his parents, that he was born blind?' (John 9:1–3). But in relation to pre-existence, the reply of Jesus was enigmatic. Two further quotations, one from the Apocrypha and one from the New Testament, are also suggestive.

> Now I was a good child by nature, and a good soul fell to my lot. Nay, rather, being good, I came into a body undefiled.
>
> Wisdom of Solomon 8:19

> Him that overcometh will I make a pillar in the temple of my God, and he shall go no more out: . . .
>
> Revelation 3:12

Why then did the idea of reincarnation disappear? The formal answer is that belief in reincarnation was made anathema, explicitly or by implication, in 553. But the background to this anathematisation is not reassuring. The Roman emperor Justinian, who was very much under the influence of his wife Theodora, a questionable character, convened at Constantinople in 543 a local synod which condemned the teachings of Origen. In 553 Justinian issued his anathemas, among them the doctrine of the pre-existence of the soul. That he submitted his anathemas for final ratification at an extra-conciliary session of the Fifth Ecumenical Council is uncertain. But if he did the background to this Council is not very propitious. With the exception of six Western Bishops from Africa, the Council was attended entirely by Oriental Bishops, no representative from Rome being present. Although Pope Vigilius was in Constantinople at the time, he refused to attend. The president of the Council was Eutychius, Patriarch of Constantinople. Against such a background it seems unlikely that the anathemas can be attributed to the work of the Holy Spirit.[51]

Sub-Section 3.   Concluding Comment

One argument, frequently and justifiably advanced against a reincarnationist hypothesis, is the tremendous expansion of world population during the last few hundred years. Where have they come from?

That there is no clear cut answer to this question is obvious, but the following observations should be borne in mind. During the last fifty years, the date of arrival of *homo sapiens* has been pushed further and further back in time. The current view, depending partly on how *sapiens* is defined, places his arrival at somewhere between 3.5 and 5 million years ago. As a result of the work of archaeologists it has become progressively evident that past civilisations were both more numerous and more extensive than was thought to be the case twenty-five years ago. And discoveries continue. Moreover, some of these civilisations indicate a knowledge of astronomy and of how to move vast blocks of stone which is most extraordinary. Where did such knowledge come from? Is there, after all, something factual in the legend of Atlantis?

In *The Hidden Wisdom in the Holy Bible*,[52] Geoffrey Hodson says:

> The Troana Manuscript, which appears to have been written about 2500 years ago among the Mayans of Yucatan and has been translated by Le Plongeon, gives the following description of the submergence of a continent in the Atlantic, presumably the Poseidonis referred to by Plato: 'In the year of 6 Kan, on the 11th Muluc in the Zac, there occurred terrible earthquakes, which continued without interruption until the 13th Chuen. The country of the hills was covered by mud, the land of Mu was sacrificed; being twice upheaved it suddenly disappeared during the night, the basin being continually shaken by volcanic forces. Being confined, these caused the land to sink and to rise several times and in various places. At last the surface gave way and ten countries were torn asunder and scattered. Unable to stand the force of the convulsions, they sank with 64,000,000 of their inhabitants 8,060 years before the writing of this book.'
>
> In a later find of an ancient Mayan manuscript known as *The Book of Chilam Balam*, discovered by A. M. Bolic, a flood is referred to thus: 'and then in one watery blow, came the waters . . . the sky fell down and the dry land sank'.

That the earth has undergone changes of a cataclysmic nature, not once but many times, is clear from data collected by I. Velikovsky and published in his book *Ages in Chaos*.[53]

Such reincarnationist traditions with which the writer is familiar affirm that until quite recently the period between incarnations was very much greater, perhaps on average twenty times greater, than the time spent in incarnation. And could it be that of the world's teeming millions many are joining the school of life on this planet for the first time? So little is known for certain that it is as well to preserve a very open mind.

References

1. *The Human Situation*, W. Macneile Dixon, (Edward Arnold & Co., 1946. First published 1937), p. 431
2. *The Implications of the Paranormal*, D. M. A. Leggett, (First 'Leggett' lecture, University of Surrey, April 1977)
3. *Out-of-the-Body Experiences*, Celia Green, (Institute of Psychophysical Research, Oxford, 1968), p. 17
4. See, for example, *A Cross-cultural Study of Beliefs in Out-of-the-body Experiences*, Dean Shiels, (*Journal*, Society for Psychical Research, March 1978), Vol. 49, No. 775
5. *The Study and Practice of Astral Projection*, Robert Crookall, (Aquarian Press, 1961), Case No. 150, p. 133
6. *Ibid*. Case No. 144, p. 129
7. *Ibid*. Case No. 126, p. 120
8. *Ibid*. Case No. 51, p. 50
9. *Ibid*. Case No. 40, p. 36
10. *Journeys out of the Body*, Robert A. Monroe, (Doubleday & Co. Inc., New York, 1971), Chap. 3, p. 55
11. *Life After Life*, Raymond A. Moody, (Bantum edition, Bantum Books Inc., New York, 1976)
12. *Reflections on Life after Life*, Raymond A. Moody, (Corgi edition, Transworld Publishers, 1978)
13. *The Boy Who Saw True*, (Neville Spearman, 1974. First published 1953), p. 144
14. *The Silent Road*, W. Tudor Pole, (Neville Spearman, 1972. First published 1960), p. 10

15. *The Unfinished Autobiography of Alice A. Bailey*, (Lucis Press, 1951), p. 35
16. *C. G. Jung: Psychological Reflections*, Jolande Jacobi, (Routledge & Kegan Paul, 1971), p. 323
17. *1957, Markings*, Dag Hammarskjöld. Translated by Leif Sjoberg and W. H. Auden. (Faber & Faber, 1964), p. 136
18. *Entia non sunt multiplicanda sine necessitate*
19. *Journal*, (American Society for Psychical Research, Jan. 1907), p. 50
20. *At the Hour of Death*, Karlis Osis and Erlendur Haraldsson, (Avon Books, New York, 1977)
21. *Swan on a Black Sea*, Geraldine Cummins, (Routledge & Kegan Paul, 1970. First published 1965), Script 39
22. *Survival of Death*, Paul Beard, (Psychic Press Ltd., 1966), Chap. 2, p. 27
23. *The City Temple Tidings*, Rev. Leslie Weatherhead. (May, 1953)
24. See, *Research into the evidence of man's survival after death. A historical and critical survey with a summary of recent developments*, Ian Stevenson, *et al.*, (*Journal of Nervous and Mental Disease*, September, 1977)
25. *The Supreme Adventure*, Robert Crookall, (Published for The Churches' Fellowship for Psychical Study by James Clarke & Co., 1961), pp. 39, 40, 42, 43
26. *Living On*, Paul Beard, (George Allen & Unwin, 1980)
27. *Survival*, David Lorimer, (Routledge & Kegan Paul, 1984)
28. *A Woman of Spirit*, Doris Collins, (Granada, 1983)
29. *The Country Beyond*, Jane Sherwood, (Neville Spearman, 1969)
30. *Testimony of Light*, Helen Greaves, (Published for The Churches' Fellowship for Psychical & Spiritual Studies by The World Fellowship Press, 1969. Republished by Neville Spearman)
31. Same as ref. 1, p. 433
32. Translation given in *The Light of the Soul*, Alice A. Bailey, (Lucis Publishing Co., New York, 1927), Book III, Sutra 18
33. *The Problem of Rebirth*, Ralph Shirley, (Rider & Co., 1936), Chap. 5
34. *The Evidence for Survival from Claimed Memories of*

Former Incarnations, Ian Stevenson, (American Society for Psychical Research, 1961), p. 17

35. *Ibid.* p. 8
36. *Twenty Cases Suggestive of Reincarnation*, Ian Stevenson, (American Society for Psychical Research. First published 1966)
37. See *Cases of the Reincarnation Type*, Ian Stevenson. Vol. I. *Ten Cases in India*, (1975). Vol. II. *Ten Cases in Sri Lanka*, (1976), (University Press of Virginia, Charlottesville, U.S.A.)
38. *Second Time Round*, E. W. Ryall, (Neville Spearman, 1974)
39. *The Wheel of Rebirth*, H. K. Challoner, (First published by Rider & Co., 1935. Republished by The Theosophical Publishing House, 1969)
40. (i) *Many Mansions*, Gina Cerminara, (Neville Spearman, 1967)
    (ii) *The World Within*, Gina Cerminara, (C. W. Daniel Company, 1973)
41. *Many Lifetimes*, Joan Grant and Denys Kelsey, (Corgi Books, 1976. First published 1969)
42. *Life before Life*, Helen Wambach, (Bantum Books, 1979)
43. *The Cathars and Reincarnation*, Arthur Guirdham, (Neville Spearman, 1970)
44. *We are One Another*, Arthur Guirdham, (Neville Spearman, 1974)
45. Same as ref. 29, p. 138
46. Same as ref. 30, p. 83
47. *Reincarnation in World Thought*, Joseph Head and S. L. Cranston, (Julian Press, Inc., New York, 1967)
48. *Reincarnations – An East–West Anthology*, Joseph Head and S. L. Cranston, (Julian Press, Inc., New York, 1961)
49. *Reincarnation: The Phoenix Fire Mystery*, Joseph Head and S. L. Cranston, (Julian Press/Crown Publishers, Inc., New York, 1977)
50. Origen, *Contra Celsum*; Bk 7, Chap. 32. *De Principiis*; Bk 1, Chaps 4, 7, 8. Bk 2, Chaps 9, 10. Bk 3, Chaps 1, 3, 21. Bk 4, Chaps 3, 4
51. See *The Hidden History of Reincarnation*, Noel Langley,

88

FROM THE PARANORMAL

(Published for The Edgar Cayce Foundation by the A.R.E. Press, U.S.A., 1965)

52. *The Hidden Wisdom in the Holy Bible*, Vol. II, Geoffrey Hodson, (Quest Books, Wheaton, U.S.A., 1969), p. 191
53. *Ages in Chaos*, I. Velikovsky, (Abacus edition, Sphere Books, 1973)

Part III
What the Evidence Indicates

6: Some Propositions

He saw the lightning in the East and longed for the East. Had he seen it in the West he would have longed for the West. But I, seeking only the lightning and its glory, care nothing for the quarters of the earth.[1]

Hermetic saying

By identifying the new learning with heresy, you make orthodoxy synonymous with ignorance.[2]

Erasmus

Life and feelings are too swift runners for us to run alongside them unless we have as guide a pace-maker, intuition, which is swift as any.[3]

A.E.

All things can be known in the vivid light of the intuition.[4]
Aphorisms of Patanjali

Before we start to draw deductions from the preceding evidence, there are three general matters which merit attention.

(i) Form and Consciousness

On looking at the world around us, we notice that everything that is alive, be it vegetable, animal, or human, manifests through a form. So far as is known life without form does not occur, and form, unless it is animated by a co-ordinating life, is always in process of disintegration.[5] So whatever lives can be studied either from the standpoint of consciousness, awareness, the capacity to respond, or from the standpoint of form or structure. Moreover, this applies not only to individual units but to communities as well. Any group, be it small, for example a school, or large, for example a nation, can be considered from the standpoint of form or structure or from the standpoint of consciousness, awareness, the capacity to respond. Form or structure, being quantitative, can be measured; consciousness or awareness, being qualitative, cannot. Hence the prevailing tendency to concentrate on measuring aspects of form or structure and to ignore consideration of consciousness or awareness.

Life on this planet has evolved over millions of years.[6] The forms through which life manifests have become progressively more complex, and the range of awareness of manifested life has both broadened and deepened.[7] The questions which naturally spring to mind are: Has the evolutionary process come to an end, or is it still going on? Are there higher – higher in the sense of more inclusive – levels of consciousness to which humanity may one day aspire? And is the human organism becoming more sensitive and so making the attainment of higher levels of consciousness possible?

(ii) Matter

Ultimately, matter is an intensely complex energy pattern. Such patterns do not always interact. Like waves on water they may pass through each other without interference. This implies that there is nothing inherently impossible about the existence of different grades of matter, or about one grade of matter passing without interference through another grade of matter.

What happens when we see? Considering light as an electromagnetic wave pattern, the eye receives and responds to some of these waves. Then, in an amazing manner, the waves are transformed and fed into the brain as electric impulses. The next thing that happens is a miracle. Somewhere, somehow, quantity is changed into quality. Electric impulses become what I see before me now, a room full of objects. What would I see if, by chance or training, I was able to receive, transform and interpret waves from a different wave band? One does not know. But it is at least possible that a different or at least extended world would come into view. If it is maintained that this has already been done, in the case of X-ray and infra-red photography, the answer is that though these provide new and interesting information, what is seen when we look at the negatives is limited to that to which our eyes, however much aided by instruments, can respond; i.e. to what lies within the range of the normal light spectrum. What lies outside this range we cannot tell.

Imagine that you have in front of you a transistor radio. By turning the appropriate dial you can tune in to one of a number of different stations. This means that several programmes – several distinct 'worlds of sound' – exist at the same point in space and at the same moment in time. Yet there is no confusion because of the radio's capacity to select, i.e. to receive and to interpret one programme at a time.

Occasionally some writers and speakers refer to the existence of a fourth dimension – and I do not mean time. If this implies the existence of four mutually perpendicular directions, I beg leave to doubt it. If, however, an interior dimension is what is meant, cf. the analogy with the transistor radio, the concept may well be sound. For too long have we allowed current thinking to block the mouth of the cave to which we are confined by the five physical senses.

(iii)   Cycles

It seems that nature abhors not only a vacuum but also straight lines. Apart from light which for all practical purposes does travel in a straight line, most things in nature behave cyclically: the alternation of day and night, the procession of the seasons, the rhythms of the body, the ebb and flow of life. Individuals have their period of growth, reach their zenith, and then decline. And the same is true of nations and of civilisations. Learning, too, takes place in a cyclic manner, the growth of knowledge and understanding resembling the distance reached by the waves on an incoming tide. So often we think of 'steady progress' and the straight line on a chart as the desirable norm. Desirable it may be, but it is not, in general, nature's norm.

Now what deductions can we draw from the data presented in Part II? What does it *suggest*? The use of the word suggest is deliberate and important, because our aim is to formulate a working hypothesis, not to prove a hypothesis already formulated. Drawing deductions is not a matter of formal logic but of personal judgement, and in the opinion of the writer the following propositions are what the evidence indicates.

1. Man is not just five pounds' worth of chemicals and a lot of water.
2. Man, when alive, can function as a self-conscious being independently of his physical body.
3. Man's consciousness survives the death of his physical body.
4. In the post-physical death state man undergoes some kind of judgement/review of the life just ended.
5. Man evolves through a series of lives, the circumstances of which are interconnected.
6. Love, justice, and perfection exist at the heart of the universe.
7. Unity underlies all that is.

As already stated the above propositions are what the writer considers the evidence implies; they are not propositions which the writer is claiming the evidence proves.

References

1. *The Occult Way*, P. G. Bowen, (The Occult Book Society, 1938), p. 222
2. Quoted on first page of *The Modern Churchman*
3. *Song and its Fountains*, A.E., (Macmillan & Co., 1932), p. 100

4. Translation given in *The Light of the Soul*, Alice A. Bailey, (Lucis Publishing Company, 1927), Book III, Sutra 33
5. This implies that livingness works against the mechanistically universal rule that, with the passage of time, there is increase in disorder
6. See *The Phenomenon of Man*, Pierre Teilhard de Chardin, (Collins, 1959)
7. In *Intelligence came first*, edited by E. Lester Smith, (The Theosophical Publishing House, Wheaton, U.S.A., 1975), the authors show conclusively that life could not have evolved *by chance*. Hence the book's title

7: The Purpose of Human Life I

For lo! the wind was blusterous
And flattened out his favourite tree;
And things looked bad for him and we –
Looked bad, I mean, for he and us –
I've never known them wuss.

Then Piglet thought a thing:
'Courage!' he said, 'There's always hope.'[1]
The House at Pooh Corner

I asked God for strength, that I might achieve – I was made weak, that I might learn humbly to obey.

I asked for help that I might do greater things – I was given infirmity that I might do better things.

I asked for riches that I might be happy – I was given poverty that I might be wise.

I asked for all things, that I might enjoy life – I was given life that I might enjoy all things.

I got nothing that I asked for – but everything I had hoped for.

Despite myself, my prayers were answered. I am, among all men, most richly blessed.
An Unknown Soldier, a century ago.

All that is exists for the sake of the soul.[2]
The Aphorisms of Patanjali

The propositions stated at the end of the preceding chapter indicate that human life is purposive, to an end that is glorious; and that progress towards this end takes place in a cyclic manner.

To illustrate what this may involve we shall consider two allegories, drawn from the experience (a) of school, (b) of learning to drive a car.

First, school. And we will begin by noting some characteristics which all schools have in common. Terms and holidays follow each other in ordered sequence throughout the whole of the time that the boy or girl is at school. During the first few terms at school the boy or girl has little say about the form or sets in which he or she is put. But as terms pass and progress is made, the boy or girl, in consultation with the staff, has increasing say about the course to be pursued and the time to be spent on different subjects. At appropriate stages in the course there are examinations to be sat. If these are not passed, they have often to be retaken. A point of some importance is to notice the extent to which specialisation takes place. Not even the most brilliant pupil is expected to be, or indeed can be, proficient at everything. Nor for that matter are the staff.

Shortly after the start of each holiday an important event occurs – the arrival of the report which reviews progress made during the term just finished. If the term's progress has been satisfactory the subsequent holiday is likely to be a period of enjoyable recreation, and of assimilating, albeit largely unconsciously, what has been learnt during the preceding term. If examinations are looming or because of innate keenness, the boy or girl may, of their own free-will, do work which will help them in the forthcoming term. This is then likely to be spent doing more advanced work, maybe in a higher form or set. If, however, the term's progress has been unsatisfactory, the holiday is likely to be marred by having to do work which may well prove uncongenial in order to make good opportunities lost during the preceding term.

Now consider what happens during a particular term. The form and sets in which the boy or girl is placed depend on three main factors. What the boy or girl has already learnt at the school; the boy or girl's capacity to learn, as exemplified by past progress; and what the boy or girl wants to do in the future. Assuming that form and sets have been settled and that term is under way, there are two points which warrant attention. First, the framework of the pupil's life at school is largely laid down. Classes and sundry other activities take place at appointed times over which the pupil has little or no control; free-will is severely restricted. Where, however, there is little or no external constraint and the pupil has almost complete free-will is in his actions and reactions within the prescribed framework. Is a particular lesson – and not just lessons – something to be enjoyed, to be resented, to be learnt from, or to be slept through? About this – *his attitude of mind* – the pupil has complete freedom. And it is this which will determine the term's progress, and what happens subsequently.

On leaving school, perhaps after a short spell as prefect, the great majority of the boys and girls go into a job or enter institutions of further education. But one or two may join the staff, either at once or after an interval. Every school has a Head who, though not permanent, often remains at the school for a somewhat longer period than the boys or girls.

In this allegory terms correspond to lives lived in physical incarnation, and holidays to the periods between. The termly report has its parallel in the review/judgement which follows each incarnation. What is likely to happen if the 'term's report' is unsatisfactory is brought out very clearly by the fate of 'the Mistress' in *The Wheel of Eternity*.[3] About 'the course to be pursued', i.e. the plan for the next incarnation, note the extract from *The Testimony of Light* quoted on p. 81 of Chapter 5.

On a cosmic time scale maybe the school has not been in existence all that long and is still in process of building up, so that the great majority of the boys and girls are in the second and third forms, and the number in the fifth and sixth forms, the forms in which examinations are taken, is still very small. Examinations raise the question of 'initiations'. While there is doubtless much truth in the adage, 'Those who know don't speak; those who speak don't know', what is said in *Initiation, Human and Solar*[4] for which Alice Bailey acted as amanuensis is, to say the least, suggestive. That the first four initiations are referred to as the Birth, Baptism, Transfiguration, and Crucifixion or Great Renunciation Initiations, prompts reflection.

The extent to which man has free-will is a question which has haunted him since he first began to think. And there is still no clear cut answer. At school, there is comparatively little freedom regarding the actual framework of time table, classes, games, meals, etc., but a great deal of freedom in respect of the boy or girl's attitude of mind in relation to what happens within the framework. Perhaps everyday life is not dissimilar. Not a great deal of freedom about what actually happens, but a great deal of freedom as to how we react to what happens – our attitude of mind. Just as at school, may it be this which progressively determines our future, both short and long term?

In relation to the allegory there remain two important questions. What is the purpose of the school of life? And who are the staff? To the first question, the answer which suggests itself is 'To educate its pupils to perform whatever parts they are called upon to play in the drama of life with grace, skill, and selfless dedication.' Or, expressed more succinctly, 'To become masters of the art and science of living.' To the second question a possible answer is 'Some of those who have passed through the school, or some comparable school, successfully.' What is involved in these answers will be considered in more detail later.

The concept of reincarnation is fraught with difficulties,[5] and one of the most serious is contained in the question 'What is it that links one life with another?' If I say that I studied magic in Egypt many centuries ago, what does the statement mean? In what sense is the I of today the I which studied magic in Egypt? At this juncture it is pertinent to ask a similar question in relation to one's present life. A snapshot in the family photograph album of a group taken fifty or more years ago. 'Yes, there I am, with my mother on one side and Uncle James on the other. That's me all right, I remember the occasion well.' In what sense is the I of today

101

the I of fifty or more years ago? What is the same? The short answer is only the consciousness of I; everything else has changed. Before returning to the difficult question of 'What is it that links one life with another,' we will reflect on a further allegory – learning to drive a car.

To begin with the learner concentrates exclusively on the mechanics of driving a particular car – steering, gear changing, use of clutch. Initially, these processes absorb the learner's complete attention, and driving along a road is not yet possible (Stage 1). But as lessons proceed, steering, changing gear, and use of clutch, gradually become automatic, and the learner is free to devote his attention to coping with the simpler hazards of normal driving (Stage 2). As progress continues the process of normal driving itself tends to become automatic, and when this happens the learner's attention is available for conversation or reflection (Stage 3). Before each of the earlier lessons the instructor decides the route, and from among the cars in the garage, selects the one in which the learner is to practice. Subsequently, car and route are decided by the instructor in consultation with the learner. After each lesson the learner reviews his performance as noted by his instructor.

In this allegory each driving lesson corresponds to an incarnation, and for the purposes of the allegory each lesson is on a different car. The handling characteristics differ markedly from one car to another, as the end in view is for the learner to become an expert driver of many types of car under very varied conditions. To provide the necessary experience some of the cars may even be defective. During any particular lesson the learner can draw upon the experiences undergone and skills acquired in earlier lessons. A near miss or accident during one lesson may manifest as fear in another.

We shall now consider the state of consciousness which corresponds to each of the three stages of learning to drive a car. Exclusive concentration on the mechanics of driving – changing gear, use of clutch, etc. – is Stage 1, and corresponds to self-centred personality awareness. Little or no thought is given to whether life has meaning. Actually driving, with awareness completely focussed on the process, is Stage 2. This corresponds to a more extensive consciousness, in which 'I wish or I want, or I don't wish or I don't want, for myself' no longer has pride of place. Instead, the dominant concern is for the well-being of the whole; though appreciation of what this involves, of what the plan for humanity may be, is only partial. Dedicated followers of great traditions are often at this stage. Driving, but talking or thinking at the same time, is Stage 3, and corresponds to the life of the spirit. For one who has arrived at this stage the plan for humanity stands revealed, and life's purpose is to further realisation of the plan with imagination, devotion, insight and love. Reaching Stage 3 corresponds in the allegory of school to being in the fifth or sixth form. But even today I suspect that the number who have reached this stage is very small. Note this statement in *A Treatise on White Magic*:

> The world cycle will cover a vast period of time. There are only about 400 accepted disciples in the world at this time (1934) – that is, men and women who really know they are disciples and know what their work is and are doing it. There are nevertheless many hundreds (out of the present generation of young people) who stand on the verge of acceptance, and thousands are upon the probationary path.[6]

In *Discipleship in the New Age*, Djwhal Khul remarks:

> I presume you will recognise the truth of what I say when I express the opinion that your individual or personal love of humanity and the focus of your attention upon human need is very largely theoretical. It is transitory and experimental in practice. Your intentions are good and fine but you have not yet the *habit* of correct orientation and much that you do is the result of hopeful endeavour . . . But the time will come when you are personally so decentralised that automatically the sense of 'others' is far stronger in you than the sense of personality or of the lower self.[7]

The consciousness of most of mankind is spread between Stages 1 and 2. Attention is so completely taken up with mastering the mechanics of driving that little is left over for considering the signposts on the road. For people at this stage it is not until the lesson is over, i.e. after death, that attention can be focussed on the meaning and direction of the life just lived. For a minority it is different, and there are doubtless a few who are approaching Stage 3. Returning to the question 'What is it that links one life with another?', for example a life lived in Egypt many centuries ago with a life lived in England today, let us see what the question becomes in terms of the allegory of learning to drive a car. The life lived in Egypt might correspond to the lesson in which the learner is being taught to start his car on an incline; while the life lived today might correspond to the lesson in which the learner is practising parking his car in a prescribed space. The lessons are so different, and the attention required so complete, that the learner, when parking, will give little or no conscious thought to the lesson devoted to starting the car on an incline. Available for use, however, will be his skill with the clutch acquired in the course of the earlier lesson. Not until the more advanced stage of driving along a road is reached will the learner have the attention available – and then only sometimes – to recall, if he so wishes, the details of his earlier lessons. And where is the knowledge and skill acquired in each lesson stored? The answer must surely be 'in the learner's mind'. But to have conscious access to its contents, he must not be so completely preoccupied with what he is learning at a particular moment that no attention is available for anything else. Turning now from the allegory to actual living, we are faced with the crucially important question 'What is it in real life which corresponds in the allegory to the learner's mind?' The answer is a centre of consciousness which transcends physical sensing, emotional feeling, and discursive thinking – the person's soul. What follows is an account of some observations by a Teacher[8] about the nature of the soul.

THE PURPOSE OF HUMAN LIFE I

The soul has three attributes. Past memory; present knowledge; and a sense of purpose.

First, memory. The soul is the storehouse of memory. During its spells in incarnation, every experience, whether good or evil, of progress or of failure, is remembered. So too are good deeds and bad deeds, fulfilments and non-fulfilments. But it is the soul which remembers, not the personality [here defined as comprising physical body, emotional nature, and discursive intellect]. Sometimes the soul lets forth a portion of its knowledge, and the personality draws into itself that knowledge. This is rare in people with little development, but for those who have learned to meditate, to still the busy conscious mind and listen, the soul begins to open, and a channel is formed between soul and personality. Memories may then flood into the personality. But when this happens it is for a purpose. The soul may wish the personality to face up to the unpleasant realities of a particular situation, or to acquire deeper understanding, or to receive greater inspiration and intuition. For most of what passes for inspiration and intuition is recalling from the soul knowledge learned in some previous incarnation. Nothing is lost in any venture into incarnation. The soul remembers and recalls at will. It is the personality that draws the blind and says, 'I do not want to know.'

Next, present knowledge. For the soul has knowledge of a kind which the personality, confined to matter and to earthly conditions, has not got. When the personality is aligned with the soul, greater knowledge becomes available to the personality. For the soul is fully conversant with the life plan of the personality which it inhabits, with what the personality came to do. The soul is not apart from the personality, though of this the personality is unaware. It therefore behoves the personality to strive to learn from the soul, and to allow the soul to control, to guide, to oversee the personality. The Ajna Chakra,[9] the centre between the eyebrows, is the seat of the soul, and it is through that centre that the personality receives inspiration and intuition.

So much that is written is written from the intellect. The words are dead words, uninspired, and fail to draw forth from the reader that raising of the consciousness into another realm that flows from the union of soul and personality. This is why poets, perhaps without realising the source of their inspiration, are able to produce poems which appeal to the heart, mind, and soul of their readers. Such is inspiration, such is intuition. When, later, the personality and soul are at one, the spirit can come flooding in. But it is only via the soul that the spirit can flood into the personality.

Finally, a sense of purpose. The soul remembers the past and is in touch with the future. It is the instrument of purpose. The soul knows the pathway you should tread, the work you should do, and the progress you are here to make. It knows where your difficulties lie, and where are your opportunities. The Master Jesus said 'Take no thought for the morrow.' If you are working with the soul, you need truly take no thought for the material morrow, for the morrow will be brought into the pattern and purpose for which the soul has incarnated. If the personality fails to make contact with the soul, it will skid off the path and lose its way. The personality may turn aside and a great opportunity could be lost. The soul knows the plan for your life, and wants you to follow the purpose which is the Will of God, the Will of the Creator, for you. Is it not written that the hairs of your head are numbered? How much more then must the soul know of the plan and purpose of your lives?

To prove the truth or falsity of the preceding commentary is, of course, impossible. What is stated will either ring true, or not ring true, for any particular reader. But the following quotations are suggestive:

From *Song and its Fountains*

There grew up the vivid sense of a being within me seeking a foothold in the body, trying through intuition and vision to create wisdom there, through poetry to impose its own music upon speech, through action trying to create an ideal society, and I was smitten with penitence because I had so often been opaque to these impulses and in league with satyr or faun in myself for so many of my days.[10]

A.E.

King Henry VI, Act 2, Scene 3

No, no, I am but shadow of myself:
You are deceiv'd, my substance is not here;

THE PURPOSE OF HUMAN LIFE I

For what you see is but the smallest part
And . . . were the whole frame here,
It is of such a spacious lofty pitch,
Your roof were not sufficient to contain it.

William Shakespeare (1564–1616)

Paracelsus, Scene 1

There is an inmost centre in us all
Where truth abides in fulness; and around,
Wall upon wall, the gross flesh hems it in,
This perfect, clear perception – which is truth.
A baffling and perverting carnal mesh
Binds it, and makes all error, and 'to know'
Rather consists in opening out a way
Whence the imprisoned splendour may escape,
Than in effecting entry for a light
Supposed to be without.

Robert Browning (1812–89)

From *The Wheel of Rebirth*[11]

Every opportunity for happiness as well as progress is given to the evolving man and the circumstances in which he is born correspond to whatsoever side of his nature he is seeking to develop. The whole object of the law of Reincarnation is that the true self shall eventually learn to create a vehicle of consciousness through which it may mirror forth every aspect of its divinity in perfect equilibrium. It is as if it were seeking to polish a mighty diamond – the true diamond soul – with a thousand facets. To do this it is forced to work in many forms, through many groups of people, to sound its note in many keys, perfecting now one side, now the other. At its best its manifestations in human form can never be more than partial – the restrictions of the body are too great. That is why it is well never to judge another, however low or ignorant he may seem to be; for he may be a great soul working out mistakes in a humble disguise.[12]

It is no more necessary that you should be burdened by the remembrance of all the events by which you gained the qualities which make you what you are, than that you should keep in your consciousness every detailed hour of your school life and

107

all the childish episodes in which you were taught the common-place decencies of life. It would do you no good to live perpetually in such a lumberhouse. But actually, nothing is forgotten. Man's unconscious mind is that lumberhouse of rejected memories while his super-conscious holds the inventory of it all and the key to the right utilization of everything there, however small and unregarded.[13]

It is likely that the existence and nature of the soul (as developed in this chapter) will strike many readers as strange. But when evidence drawn from many different traditions (see also the quotation from the *Mundake Upanishad* on p. 149, Chapter 10) all points in the same direction, the probability that the direction is right builds up.

A matter which now comes up for consideration is how does one incarnation affect another? What determines the conditions of a particular life, its physical environment and the character and endowments of the personality? Given that human life is purposive, this can scarcely be a matter of pure chance. To affirm that it all depends on the genes may be true, but that is only one link in the chain. What determines the arrangement of the genes? Assuming that there is some connection between one life and another, where can we look for guidance?

The answer which suggests itself is the religious traditions of East and West, and certain data from paranormal sources. In Buddhism and Hinduism, karma, defined as the law of cause and effect or ethical causation, is the subject of a vast literature. But little of it sheds much light on the practical question of what determines the physical environ-ment and the character and endowments of the personality in a particular incarnation. In Christianity there is even less as reincarnation is not part of the orthodox Christian tradition, but the saying of Christ recorded in each of the first three Gospels is highly significant: 'For with what measure ye mete it shall be measured to you again.'

Of data from paranormal sources there is not a lot, but there is some.

First Edgar Cayce. As pointed out earlier, Edgar Cayce had given upwards of 2500 'life readings' by the time of his death, and many of these purported to show how a person's present difficulties stemmed from how he or she had acted in a previous life. What follows are three examples, taken from *Many Mansions* by Gina Cerminara.[14]

A woman of forty-five, wife of a professional man and mother of three children was stricken at the age of thirty-six with infantile paralysis and has not walked since. Her life is lived in a wheelchair; she is completely dependent on others for transportation to any point outside the home. The karmic cause is attributed by the reading to the entity's behaviour in ancient Rome. She had been among the royalty of the time, and was closely associated with Nero in his persecution of the Christians. 'And the entity laughed at those who were crippled in the arena' – says the reading – 'and lo! that selfsame thing returns to you!'[15]

A woman – a divorcée in her late thirties – with a completely uninhibited personality is currently preoccupied with her third matrimonial venture. The basis for her vivacious social competence was, according to the Cayce reading, laid in two past lives: one as a dance-hall entertainer in early frontier days; another as one of the mistresses of Louis XIV in the court of France. From the latter experience came her gifts of diplomacy and fascination, and the ability, as the reading puts it, 'to wind everyone around her finger, from king to scullery maid'. As a dance-hall entertainer she capitalized on these gifts and developed them still further, until a reversal of fortunes and a change of heart led her to become a kind of ministering angel in her community.[16]

All his life a food inspector in the Navy has had a consuming interest in stones and gems; he founded a gem exchange and has always been closely associated with gem cutters and collectors. Since retirement from the Navy, he has devoted all his time to this interest – further stimulated to do so by the strange encouragement given him by his Cayce reading. His past lives were given as follows: first, as a trader in trinkets and firewater with the Indians in Ohio; second, as a merchant in Persia, who travelled by caravan and dealt in the linens of Egypt, the pearls of Persia, the opal, firestone, and lapis lazuli of Indo-China, and the diamonds and rubies of the Cities of Gold; third, as a Hittite in the Holy Land who provided the precious stones used in the garments of the priests.[17]

Next, some extracts from the Teacher's comments in *The Wheel of Rebirth*.

No one – unless he can read not only man's past but even the world Karma of the moment – is able to see the true cause of contemporary events. But we take a wider view. We see things in a better perspective since we can look forward as well as back, and consider the overall plan to be of greater importance than the individual. You must realize, moreover, that there is such a thing as national, racial and even planetary Karma to be taken into consideration. You are too inclined to think of Karma as only applicable to the life of man; but man's life fits into the pattern of greater lives, even as the little cellular lives in your body are part of your own physical state. The consideration of such intricate workings of the One Law may well make your finite mind reel, but at least it can teach you, if it does nothing more, not to be too hasty in your superficial judgements of any occurrences, either those related to the lives of personalities or to more far-reaching events.[18]

It is curious how difficult man finds it to apply occult truths to the everyday facts of life! As I have told you, by your thoughts and deeds in one life you build the vehicle which will incorporate your spirit in the next. If you impoverish the constitution of your bodies, you will return with similarly impoverished – or almost moribund – atoms and will have to nurture and develop them afresh.[19] Thus an enfeebled mind is often the result of mental laziness or of intelligence wrongly used, and those who weaken their bodies through excess and perversion may reincarnate deformed, epileptic, with some disease, or some fault in the brain, weakness of will, and inherent tendency to their former vices through which any malignant force from their past can more easily manifest.[20]

Whatever Kingdom of nature you injure, pervert or exploit you will at some time have to reconcile to yourself through love

110

and service. Until you do there will be enmity between you; its members will be inimical – not deliberately but because you have placed yourself in opposition to them and therefore your vibrations strike a discord with theirs.[21]

Finally, a little first-hand experience. Between 1968 and 1975 the university where I worked had its share of student unrest, and its Vice-Chancellor had his share of administrative worries! At the finish, the Teacher referred to on page 121, from whom I had received help and advice, said to me 'You probably don't remember, but in a previous life you were a trouble-maker. For this reason it was essential for your development that some time, either in this life or a later one, you should experience "trouble". You can be thankful that the last few years have provided you with the opportunity to learn the lessons which this experience had to teach and so to resolve this particular aspect of your karma.'

In order to crystallise ideas there follow seven propositions which the writer feels are *suggested* by the evidence in this chapter.

1.   Man is triple: Personality, soul and spirit.
2.   The fruits of each incarnation, i.e. the qualities developed and the skills acquired, are absorbed by the soul.
3.   The soul remembers the past, is in touch with the future, and is itself evolving.
4.   Successive incarnations are interconnected in two ways. Continuity of consciousness is preserved by the soul. The conditions of a particular life, i.e. the characteristics of the personality and the material environment in which the life is lived, result from causes set in motion in previous lives.
5.   As the soul evolves the link between soul and personality grows stronger.
6.   When, in the allegory of learning to drive a car, Stage 2 is reached, the link between soul and personality is such that there comes into being a 'soul infused personality', i.e. a personality which in full consciousness is under the guidance and direction of the soul.

111

7.   Another link now starts to develop – between the soul infused personality and the spirit – the atman in Hinduism. This leads to the life of the spirit, to mastery of the art and science of living, and the end of the human journey.

References

1.   *The House at Pooh Corner*, A. A. Milne. From the Chapter 'Eeyore finds the Wolery'
2.   Translation given in *The Light of the Soul*, Alice A. Bailey, (Lucis Publishing Co., 1927), Book II, Sutra 21
3.   *The Wheel of Eternity*, Helen Greaves, (Neville Spearman, 1974)
4.   *Initiation, Human and Solar*, Alice A. Bailey, (Lucifer Publishing Co., 1922)
5.   *Death and Eternal Life*, John Hick, (Collins, 1976), Part IV
6.   *A Treatise on White Magic*, Alice A. Bailey, (Lucis Publishing Co., 5th edition, 1951. First published 1934), p. 164
7.   *Discipleship in the New Age*, Alice A. Bailey, (Lucis Press, 1955), Vol. II, p. 297
8.   See Chapter 6 of *A Forgotton Truth*, D. M. A. Leggett & M. G. Payne, (Pilgrims Book Services, 1986)
9.   See Chap. 10
10.   *Song and its Fountains*, A.E., (Macmillan and Co., 1932), p. 8
11.   *The Wheel of Rebirth*, H. K. Challoner, (Theosophical Publishing House, 1969. First published by Rider & Co., 1935)
12.   *Ibid.* p. 140
13.   *Ibid.* p. 202
14.   *Many Mansions*, Gina Cerminara, (Neville Spearman, 1967)
15.   *Ibid.* p. 64
16.   *Ibid.* p. 118
17.   *Ibid.* p. 218
18.   Same as ref. 11, p. 118
19.   This theme is developed in much greater detail by the same Teacher in *The Path of Healing*, by H. K. Challoner, (Theosophical Publishing House, 1972. First published by Rider & Co., 1938)
20.   Same as ref. 11, p. 198
21.   *Ibid.* p. 200

8: The Purpose of Human Life II

There is a natural body, and there is a spiritual body.[1]

I Corinthians

The transfer of the consciousness from a lower vehicle into a higher is part of the great creative and evolutionary process.[2]

The Aphorisms of Patanjali

Jesus saith unto him, I am the way, the truth, and the life: no one cometh unto the Father, but by me.[3]

John

The very thing that is now called the Christian religion was not wanting amongst the ancients from the beginning of the human race, until Christ came in the flesh, after which the true religion, which already existed, began to be called 'Christian'.[4]

St Augustine

We must now follow up several matters touched on in the last chapter. In particular, and in terms of the allegory of the school, what happens during holiday time, and what happens after leaving school? Consideration of these two questions quickly raises the antecedent question of levels of awareness. So we must begin by considering that.

As a matter of experience our normal consciousness moves, often with great rapidity, throughout a domain comprising physical sensing, emotional feeling and discursive thinking. Diagrammatically, the conscious self or 'I' can be represented in Figure 1 by a point P which moves within the band bounded by lines AA and BB. The question then arises 'Is the domain bounded by AA and BB all there is?'

113

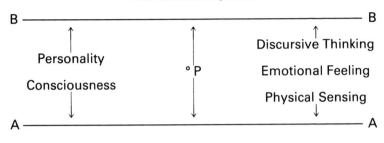

Figure 1

Poets, mystics, and certain evidence from the paranormal all give an unqualified 'No'. This inevitably prompts the next question, namely, 'What is it that lies outside the domain bounded by AA and BB, and how can it be explored?' To this question the answers are varied and for the most part tentative. Something of an exception is the concept which is held by many schools of Indian thought – see, in particular, Books I and II of the *Yoga Aphorisms of Patanjali*[5] – and is expressed diagrammatically in Figure 2.

According to this view an individual can, as a result of training and experience (which may extend over many lives) achieve soul consciousness, i.e. be able to function in the realm represented in Figure 2 as lying between BB and CC. This ability is, of course, additional to, not instead of, the capacity to function in the domain lying between AA and BB.

Although using a two-dimensional diagram to represent something which is by analogy multidimensional is dangerous, it is not entirely without value so long as the limitations in so doing are not lost sight of.

In Chapter 6 we saw that there was nothing inherently impossible about the concept and existence of different grades of matter. That the five physical senses require for their functioning physical matter is self evident. But what is the situation in relation to experiencing an emotion or

114

D ——————————————————————— D

Divine
Consciousness

C ——————————————————————— C

Soul
Consciousness

Divine Livingness

Intuitive Wisdom and Union

Spiritual Insight and Understanding

B ——————————————————————— B

Personality
Consciousness

Discursive Thinking

Emotional Feeling

Physical Sensing

A ——————————————————————— A

Figure 2

conceiving a thought? Do these functions imply the
existence of emotional matter and mental matter? The
Indian schools of thought already referred to answer 'Yes'.
On this basis the space occupied by the earth and its
neighbourhood will contain matter of many different grades:
physical, emotional, mental, and maybe other grades as
well. Moreover, if it is assumed that each grade of matter is
subject to attraction, to gravitation, it follows that the
various grades of matter will tend to arrange themselves in
the manner shown in Figure 3, each sphere representing the
boundary for matter of a particular grade.[6] In the figure it is
assumed that emotional matter extends beyond the limit of
physical matter, and that mental matter extends beyond
the limit of emotional matter. If, within each grade of
matter, there is matter of varying density, as is the case for

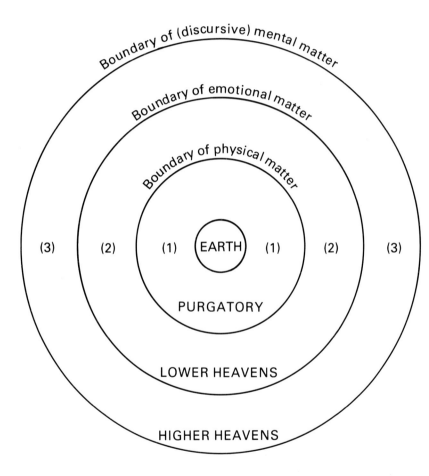

Figure 3[6] (not to scale)

physical matter, it follows that for each grade of matter density will diminish with distance from the earth's centre. If this picture is broadly correct, what are the implications for the form through which man manifests – his 'body'?[7] A natural deduction is that man's 'body' includes matter of many different grades, not just physical matter, and that it is the presence of these other grades of matter which makes it possible for man to feel, to think, and to experience other levels of awareness. Moreover, it seems reasonable to assume that the interaction which exists between the physical body and physical sensing has its counterpart at other levels, for example that there is interaction between emotional matter and emotional feeling, and between mental matter and discursive thinking. If this is the case, the consequences are important. For it means that the kind of thoughts and feelings which we habitually harbour will affect the mental and emotional matter in our 'body', and that the quality of the mental and emotional matter in our 'body' will condition our thoughts and feelings. Refined thoughts and feelings will lead to the presence in our 'body' of refined mental and emotional matter; coarse thoughts and feelings to coarse mental and emotional matter. If the foregoing analysis is sound, the rationale of the following sayings is clear:

> For as he thinketh in his heart, so he is.
>
> Proverbs 23:7

> You are not what you think you are, but what you think, you are.
>
> Source unknown

> Whatsoever things are true, whatsoever things are honest, whatsoever things are just, whatsoever things are pure, whatsoever things are lovely, whatsoever things are of good report; if there be any virtue, and if there be any praise, think on these things.
>
> Philippians 4:8

We are now in a position to consider the first of the two

questions posed at the beginning of this chapter. 'In terms of the allegory of the school, what happens during holiday time?' At death the purely physical matter in a person's 'body' is left behind, but matter of all other grades, in particular the mental and emotional matter in the 'body' is retained. Moreover the quality of this emotional and mental matter is important, because it is this which determines a person's 'location'. If the matter is coarse, and therefore 'heavy', the individual will gravitate to a 'location' which may be near, or even *under*, the earth's surface, the latter corresponding to the underworld of Greek and other mythologies. If, on the other hand, the mental and emotional matter is refined, and therefore 'light', the person's 'location' may correspond to the 'summer land' of spiritualistic communication, a location well *above* the surface of the earth. As there is no reason to suppose that mental and emotional matter is not every bit as complex as physical matter, it is virtually certain that within zones (1), (2), (3), in Figure 3 there are many different 'levels'. 'In my Father's house are many mansions [abiding places, dwelling places], if it were not so, I would have told you.'[8] What paranormal evidence also indicates is that though it is possible by an effort of the will and with adequate knowledge to descend from one's natural location to lower regions, to ascend to regions above one's natural location is not possible except under exceptional circumstances, and then only temporarily. Ascending permanently to higher regions only becomes possible as the emotional and mental matter in the 'body' is refined, and the 'body' itself is thereby 'lightened'.

The next question is 'What, after death, corresponds to the five physical senses? Is there anything analogous to seeing and hearing?' Evidence from the paranormal is unequivocal in suggesting (a) that there is an awareness comparable to physical seeing and hearing, but more intense; (b) that there are no specific organs corresponding to physical eyes or ears. That 'sensing' occurs there is no doubt, but how is a mystery. The comment in *The Light of the Soul*[5] about Sutra 30, in Book 1 of *The Yoga Aphorisms of Patanjali* states: 'Clairvoyance is the faculty of sight upon the astral plane and is one of the lower "siddhis" or psychic powers. It is achieved through a surface sensibility of the entire "body of feeling", the emotional sheath, and is sensuous perception carried to a very advanced condition.'

Assuming that there is 'sensing', what is it that is sensed? Though the question is simple, it raises acute difficulties,[9] because of the greatly enhanced facility to create in the after death conditions of existence. In ordinary life, giving effect to our desires takes time and effort. In after death conditions the effect is almost instantaneous. From this it seems clear – and there is a lot of paranormal evidence in support – that though a person's environment is not wholly subjective, it is none the less greatly and rapidly influenced by his thoughts and feelings, by his desires.[10] If a person's attitude of mind is coarse, hard and unloving, so will be his surroundings. If his attitude is refined, gentle and loving, his surroundings will reflect these qualities.

Paranormal evidence indicates that after death, conditions are no more static than are the conditions of ordinary life, and that everyone is subject to a gradual process of withdrawal – from more, to less, material conditions.[11] As each set of environing conditions is experienced and worked through, the matter in the person's 'body' appropriate for experiencing such conditions is automatically discarded. The 'body' is thus 'lightened', and so rises to a new 'location' in which the environing conditions are less material, and consciousness correspondingly less self-centred. When a person reaches the outer boundary of zone (2), it seems that a major change takes place, sometimes referred to as the second death.[12] With the discarding of all emotional matter, the individual's consciousness now awakes to the glories of the heaven world, the level of consciousness referred to in the New Testament as the Kingdom of Heaven. As already pointed out, this level of consciousness can be attained in physical incarnation when the personality is in perfect alignment with the soul. But such an achievement, which corresponds to the arrival at Stage 2 in the allegory of learning to drive a car, is rare. For all but the very few, the period of re-creation following the past life on earth now draws to a close and the soul seeks further experience of earth life by another physical incarnation.

For the very few who are able to proceed beyond zone (3), the end of the human journey is in sight, and we must consider the second of the two questions posed at the beginning of this chapter – 'In terms of the allegory, what happens after leaving school?' Although this is unlikely to be of immediate concern to most of us for a very long time to come, it is relevant to note references in various quarters to 'the higher evolution',[13] i.e. to the next stage on 'the path of return to the centre' after the purely human phase has been successfully completed. Such a picture implies that the answer to the question 'What happens after leaving school?' is, in terms of the allegory, 'Adult life'.

Until the time of Galileo it was assumed that the earth was the centre of the universe. Now, four centuries later, we know that not only is the earth not the centre of the universe, but that it is a planet of indifferent size, orbiting a not very large sun (relative to other suns), in a vast galaxy, which is one of millions. In metaphorical terms the earth is a very small pebble on a very large beach. Such a change in status in the course of a mere four centuries can only be described as striking. But strangely, there has been no comparable change in outlook regarding the status of humanity, regarded by believers as the apex of God's creation, and by non-believers as the pinnacle of evolution. Is not such an assumption very extraordinary and quite unjustified? Once it is appreciated that in terms of the allegory much of school life and the whole of adult life takes place under conditions such as those which prevail in zones (1), (2), (3), . . . in Figure 3, i.e. under conditions which are not detectable by the five physical senses, the assessment by humanity of its place in the cosmos is likely to undergo profound change. About this a Teacher[14] has made the following observation:

> There are many many planes of life. We may be on a plane some distance beyond yours, but believe me, my friend, there are planes beyond ours, far far beyond ours, of which we know very little. We know about as much of those planes as you know of ours. There are many planes, not one, hidden, as your Church tries to tell you.

By now the reader's reaction to the suggestions made in the last few pages may well be 'But this is fantastic'. Novel, and therefore strange, they may be. But before what has been hypothesised is dismissed as fantasy, let us reflect for a moment on the nature of the physical world; of the solids, liquids and gases with which we are all so familiar and which we take so much for granted. On ultimate analysis these solids, liquids and gases, are immensely complex energy patterns in space that is otherwise assumed to be empty. But this is a far cry from the table at which I am writing or the chair on which I am sitting. What is so remarkable – though not regarded as remarkable because it is happening all the time – is the capacity of the human mind to interpret energy patterns as tables and chairs replete with secondary qualities such as colour, hardness and smell. We fail to realise, or if we realise we overlook, the extent to which we live here and now in a thought created world. With this in mind, is hypothesising the existence of different energy patterns which our minds can interpret in a different way really so extraordinary? Would not a fairer appraisal of the position be surprise if it were not so?

When considering the allegory of the school, it was suggested that the staff consisted of 'some of those who have passed through the school, or some comparable school, successfully'. We must now consider the implications of this suggestion in more detail. That a school must have a staff to run it and to teach its pupils is obvious. But what is the evidence for the existence of such a staff in the case of humanity? References to 'The Inner Government of the World', 'The Guardians of the Race', 'The Hierarchy of Masters', 'The Communion of Saints', 'The Angelic Hierarchy', keep cropping up in various writings from time to time, but what is the evidence that these references reflect a reality and are not just figments in the imagination of the writers? As with the question of survival, a single piece of evidence which will prove the matter once and for all does not exist. But there is no little evidence of a less conclusive kind. What are we to make of K.H. and D.K. in Alice Bailey's *Autobiography*,[15] for example the passage quoted on page 61 in Chapter 5, the Teacher in H. K. Challoner's *Wheel of Rebirth*,[16] and the quite different Teacher in Clarice Toyne's *Testament of Truth*?[17] Did the authors of these three books imagine the Teachers they referred to who subsequently taught them? A study of the teaching which flowed from these Teachers leads to a quite definite 'No'. For much of the teaching is of a scope and of a quality that go far beyond what the authors concerned could have put forward unaided. Each of them has said so – most emphatically – and common sense supports their assertion. Though the preceding examples do not constitute proof, they do provide evidence. And when it is borne in mind that the examples cited are only three out of many, the evidence becomes significant.

Also relevant is the following first-hand experience. In 1955 the writer was invited to speak at a conference in Holland. Mr Kaiser, a fine linguist, was Chairman of the organising committee; Miss Hofmans, a noted healer, was one of its members. During the conference I asked Mr Kaiser if I could have an interview with Miss Hofmans, who didn't speak much English, with himself acting as interpreter. After agreeing to my request, he said: 'I will, of course, translate into English what Miss Hofmans will say in Dutch. But there will be no need for me to translate your English into Dutch. Provided you formulate your question clearly, Miss Hofmans will pick it up directly from your mind.' Whether this did indeed happen I was not to know as my question was a simple one linguistically for which Miss Hofmans' English may well have been adequate. But it provided an arresting start to the interview! Having asked my question about a matter that was worrying me at the time, I received a reply which, after two days' reflection, I felt was worthy of the Delphic Oracle! What was said was profoundly wise. Then followed a memorable experience, begun by Miss Hofmans saying: 'Now I have a number of things to say to you.' For the next twenty-five minutes I was stripped, metaphorically speaking, absolutely naked. What she said (a) displayed complete knowledge of my activities and of my thoughts and feelings, often of a most intimate nature, and (b) was concerned with making my work, both professional and otherwise, more effective. Effective, that is, for people I was trying to help. At the end of the interview Miss Hofmans, who was fully conscious throughout albeit in a meditative posture, said 'You appreciate that I am not speaking to you from my own wisdom. I am merely acting as a communicator for the Teacher.' Since then I have met two other people with comparable telepathic facility. One of them has 'far memory' and recollects being a Pythoness, the name given to the women communicators at Delphi.

Having regard to the existence of so much evidence of a kind similar to that just cited, it seems beyond reasonable doubt that there are indeed highly evolved souls, Teachers, far in advance of normal humanity in wisdom and understanding, who are deeply and intimately concerned with the spiritual development of mankind. Of such souls it would appear that some are incarnate and some are not. But of those who are, few if any, are known to the general public. Why? For one simple and obvious reason. Publicity would render impossible the work which they are here to do.

Having established the existence of a staff (in terms of the allegory of the school), to whom are they responsible? Is there a head? Before tackling this question an attempt must be made to answer, or at least consider, a question which has puzzled and haunted the Western World, and not only the Western World if it comes to that, for the last two thousand years. Who was Jesus? Who was Christ? The writer is not unaware of the difficulties and dangers inherent in asking such a question, but an answer is so central to our overall theme – the purpose of human life on this planet – that it cannot be bypassed.

What are the indisputable facts, if any, about the central figure in the Christian Gospel? For the writer they include the following:

(1)   An outstanding religious teacher was born, and died, in Palestine some two thousand years ago.

(2)   Almost nothing reliable is known about the first thirty years of his life.

(3)   Much more is known, although there is continuing uncertainty regarding details, about the period of his Ministry.[18] This culminated with his crucifixion at Jerusalem for claiming to be the Messiah.

(4)   Following his resurrection, he appeared in physical form to his disciples and others on a number of different occasions.

It is also notable that, following his death, there has been continuous debate about his nature. Was he man? Was he God? Was he man who became God? Was he God who became man? Was he both God and man at one and the same time? Moreover the debate continues.[19] Today, in the minds of most people, the name Christ refers to the central character in the Gospel Story – He who lived and died in Palestine two thousand years ago – and the Son, the second 'person' of the Christian Trinity – Father, Son, and Holy Spirit. But there are, in addition, phrases current such as 'The Cosmic Christ', 'Christ in you the hope of glory', 'The birth of the Christ within the heart'. And what of Jesus? Did he *become* the Christ (the anointed one) after his baptism by

124

John the Baptist? In many addresses and much writing the names Jesus and Christ are treated as interchangeable.

Having regard to the above statements, statements which are essentially factual, the writer feels moved to make the following observations:

(a)   During Jesus' childhood there is no hint that he was regarded as other than a normal boy, albeit exceptionally perceptive and intelligent – 'all that heard him were amazed at his understanding and his answers' – but not different in kind from other boys. For example, he caused what would seem to have been quite unnecessary trouble and worry to his parents by not telling them that he would be remaining behind in the temple. 'Son, why hast thou thus dealt with us? Behold, thy father and I sought thee sorrowing.' Also revealing is the observation of those who heard him when he preached at Nazareth at the beginning of his Ministry. 'Is not this Joseph's son?'[20]

(b)   The nature of Jesus' Ministry makes it inconceivable that he remained in the carpenter's shop at Nazareth until the time of his baptism by John. But where he went we do not know. A sojourn in an Essene monastery and a further visit to Egypt are obvious possibilities.

(c)   Jesus' Ministry – what he taught and the way he lived and died – had such a consistently sublime quality that it is difficult to believe that he was purely human, using the word human in its normally accepted sense. Exceptions, such as cursing the fig tree, are so few and so completely out of character that their authenticity must be regarded with the gravest suspicion.[21]

(d)   Great confusion appears to surround the empty tomb. That it was indeed empty seems virtually certain. What happened to the matter of which the body was composed we do not know. But Sutra 45 Book III of *The Aphorisms of Patanjali* is significant. Commenting on this Sutra Charles Johnston says 'The spiritual man is said to possess eight powers: (i) the atomic, the power of assimilating himself with the nature of the atom, which will, perhaps, involve the power to disintegrate material forms; . . .'[22] But, taken by itself, the empty tomb has little to do with Jesus' resurrection, if by this is meant his continued existence after death. The latter, surely, was proved by his appearances, which would use matter altogether different from the physical matter of the crucified body.[23] Cf. (a) cases (viii) and (ix) on p. 59 and 61 of Chapter 6, and case (v) on p. 67 of Chapter 6; (b) the esoteric tradition that sufficiently evolved beings can construct by an act of will their own body of manifestation.[24] But, this said, the significance of the tomb being empty remains very great. For it substantiates prophecy, demonstrates the quite exceptional nature of the life just ended, and may well be symbolic of the eventual 'redemption of matter'.

(e) A scientific or philosophic impasse nearly always implies that one or more of the basic definitions or assumptions requires amendment. Regarding the nature of Jesus the two key words are 'man' and 'God'. To 'man' we have already given a deeper meaning than is customary. What meaning can be attached to the word God will be considered in Chapter 9.

In the light of the preceding observations and the general intractability of the problem, it is tempting to look for a different approach from those normally adopted. One such approach is embodied in the occult tradition that Jesus was a high initiate who was overshadowed by, and on occasions lent his body to, the Christ, a very exalted being whose human evolution lay in the far distant past.

To the question, 'Is it possible for the physical body of a (living) human being to be used by another entity, human or not as the case may be?', there is very strong evidence that the answer is 'Yes'.

Though possession by another entity is not nearly as common as is often made out, there are few people who have worked in this very difficult field who would assert that possession never occurs. A crucial characteristic of genuine possession is that the possessing entity has seized control of a physical body contrary to the wish of that body's rightful owner.

In the case of a trance medium, the situation is different in that the medium, when in trance, is willing for his/her body to be used as a channel of communication for a discarnate being. But when in trance, the medium (as distinct from his/her control – when such exists) has little or no control over who communicates.

This leads on to consider whether it is possible for someone to step out of his body in full consciousness and let someone else, perhaps a highly evolved soul, take over? About this possibility evidence is scanty, but there is some. The writer had the privilege of knowing the late Mrs Bendit (née Phoebe Payne), a very remarkable clairvoyant, during the last fifteen years of her life. About a certain well-known speaker X to whom she had often listened, she said that when X was speaking, another being Y was usually in close proximity, and that sometimes X would vacate his body and Y would take over. Y was a highly evolved soul, and when he took over the quality of what was said went up accordingly. If this is correct, and the writer has no reason to doubt it, there are far reaching implications.

For the reader meeting this idea for the first time the idea will probably seem very strange. But it does go some way to explain some singularly difficult features of the central problem, to wit –

(i) The human quality of Jesus' early years. Until the Baptism he would be a normal human being, albeit an especially perceptive and gifted one.

(ii) The sublime quality of Jesus' Ministry. But the varying degree of overshadowing would puzzle his hearers, including maybe his disciples.

In *A Man Seen Afar* by Wellesley Tudor Pole – originator of 'the silent minute' in World War II – and

Rosamond Lehmann, there is the following passage:

> Jesus never seems to have made it clear to them (His Disciples) when he was speaking as an individual to individuals, and when the Christ was speaking through him – not so much to those present as to the countless generations yet unborn. In the middle of a conversation, often about everyday affairs, his countenance would change, his delivery become compelling, authoritative. Then the words that issued forth would be addressed to all mankind in all ages . . . But those who were actually listening went on applying his prophecies and statements solely to themselves and to their own generation.
>
> I am speaking, of course, of the three years at the close of his short life when the Christ clothed and permeated his whole being. In earlier years he was very much a man among men, speaking a language they could understand, often eloquent, inspiring, but always simple. Not until he met John the Baptist did the immensity of the mission which lay ahead begin to dawn and then gradually to encompass him.
>
> I feel certain that there are records still in existence, awaiting discovery, which will make clear the mystery of the Master's seemingly dual personality, and elucidate the change that took place within him in the waters of the Jordan, in his twenty-eighth year.[25]

(iii) The words spoken from the cross, in particular 'My God, my God, why hast thou forsaken me?'[26] These would have come from Jesus, not the Christ. About this utterance Djwhal Khul, Alice Bailey's Teacher, says:

> One tremendous experience is vouchsafed to the initiate at this time (the fourth initiation experience, usually referred to as the Crucificion or Great Renunciation Initiation, which Jesus was then undergoing). It brings to the forefront of his consciousness the sudden and appalling recognition that the soul itself, that which for ages has been the supposed source of his existence and his guide and mentor, is no longer needed; his relation, as a soul-infused personality, is now directly with the Monad (the atman in Hinduism). He feels bereft and is apt to cry out – as did the Master Jesus – 'My God, my God, why hast thou forsaken me?' At that supreme moment there was a fusion

128

of agonies. Jesus, crucified there, felt the agony of human need and renounced his own life and gave his all (symbolically speaking) to meet that need. The Christ, at that time overshadowing his great disciple, also passed simultaneously through a great initiatory experience. The agony of his yearning for revelation and increased enlightenment (in order to enhance his equipment as world saviour) revealed to him the new possibilities, from which – when confronted with them dimly in the Garden of Gethsemane and later upon the cross – His whole nature shrank.[27]

(iv)   Of the post-crucifixion appearance, some, such as to Mary Magdalene, were undoubtedly of Jesus; but perhaps not all. Some, may be, were of the Christ.

To the question raised earlier in connection with the allegory of school 'To whom are the staff responsible? Is there a head?' The answer is 'Yes, for the last two thousand years it has been the Christ, and he will hold this position "until the end of the age".'

A fitting conclusion to this section are some comments by the Teacher in *The Wheel of Rebirth*.

The teaching of Christ was the final synthesis of all that had gone before. He expounded to mankind the Perfect and Everlasting Law, not for this age and this race alone, but for every Race and for every Age. 'Love God and love thy neighbour as thyself'; 'In what measure ye mete it shall be measured to you again.' Here, in two burning sentences is the Law complete. If every cult and religion were wiped out of existence and only this remained – it would be enough; for to the man who followed this Law without shadow of turning, all other things, all knowledge, all wisdom, all power and bliss would inevitably be added.

You think now that it is impossible to live this law, to build a civilization upon it? I tell you it is not impossible. Mankind through a multitude of bitter experiments will come, one day, to the realization that life, lived as Christ taught and lived, is the only method through which happiness and harmony for the individual as well as for the race, can be attained. Men talk of the Millenium – they do not realize that Christ gave them the key to that Age of Perfection. This is not yet understood. Men prefer to look without rather than within for revelations – it is so much easier. Yet it must be understood if humanity is to be saved from fresh disasters.[28]

Six propositions are suggested by matters discussed in this chapter.

(1) Associated with this planet are many levels of consciousness and many grades of matter.

(2) Proposition (1) provides the rationale of Jesus' two statements: (i) 'The Kingdom of Heaven is within you.' (ii) 'In my Father's house are many mansions.'

(3) Such phrases as 'The Communion of Saints', 'The Hierarchy of Masters', 'The Guardians of the Race', refer to beings who have passed through this or some other school of human life.

(4) Jesus was a high initiate who was overshadowed by the Christ during the years of his Ministry in Palestine two thousand years ago.

(5) The Christ, who passed through the school of human life a long time ago, has been Head of the Hierarchy – Master of the Masters – for the last two thousand years, and will continue so to be 'until the end of the age'.

(6) There are probably many evolutionary schemes of self-conscious beings within the solar system.

References

1. 1 Corinthians 15:44
2. Translation given in *The Light of the Soul*, Alice A. Bailey, (Lucis Publishing Co., New York, 1927), Book IV, Sutra 2
3. John 14:6
4. St Augustine, Bishop of Hippo. Epis. Retract., Lib. 1, xiii. 3
5. Same as ref. 2
6. (i) 'The Location of Heaven – the Lokas and Talas of Occultism', E. L. Gardner, (Article in *The Theophist*, 1954)
    (ii) *The Imperishable Body*, E. L. Gardner, (Theosophical Publishing House, 1948), p. 20

7. See *The Play of Consciousness*, E. L. Gardner, (Theosophical Publishing House, 1939), p. 78
8. John 14:2
9. Many communicators have said '*We* have not the words, and *you* have not the concepts, to comprehend or picture our mode of existence.'
10. See Part Two of *Living On*, Paul Beard, (G. Allen & Unwin, 1980)
11. *Testimony of Light*, Helen Greaves, (Published for the Churches' Fellowship for Psychic & Spiritual Studies by the World Fellowship Press, 1969)
12. *The Next World – and the Next*, Robert Crookall, (Theosophical Publishing House, 1966)
13. *Treatise on Cosmic Fire*, Alice A. Bailey, (Lucis Press, 5th edition 1952. First published, New York, 1925), p. 1241
14. See Chapter 6 of *A Forgotten Truth*, D. M. A. Leggett & M. G. Payne, (Pilgrims Book Services, 1986)
15. *The Unfinished Autobiography of Alice A. Bailey*, (Lucis Press, 1951)
16. *The Wheel of Rebirth*, H. K. Challoner, (Theosophical Publishing House, 1969. First published by Rider & Co., 1935)
17. *The Testament of Truth*, Clarice Toyne, (Allen & Unwin, 1970)
18. *Can we trust the New Testament?*, John A. T. Robinson, (Mowbrays, 1977)
19. (i) *The Myth of God Incarnate*, Edited by John Hick, (S.C.M. Press, 1977)
    (ii) *The Truth of God Incarnate*, Edited by Michael Green, (Hodder & Stoughton, 1977)
20. Luke 4:22
21. See (i) *The New Man*, Maurice Nicoll, (Vincent Stuart, 1955. First published by Stuart and Richards, 1950); (ii) *The Hidden Wisdom in the Holy Bible*, Geoffrey Hodson, (The Theosophical Publishing House, Wheaton, U.S.A.), p. 34
22. *The Yoga Sutras of Patanjali*, an interpretation, by Charles Johnston, (J. M. Watkins, London, 1949. First published in New York, 1912)
23. See *The Easter Enigma*, Michael C. Perry, (Faber & Faber, 1959)

24. On p. 761 of ref. 13 it is stated –
    The Mayavirupa, literally the illusory form, the body of temporary manifestation which the Adept creates on occasion through the power of the will and in which He functions in order to make certain contacts on the physical plane and to engage in certain work for the race
25. *A Man Seen Afar*, Wellesley Tudor Pole and Rosamond Lehmann, (Neville Spearman, 1965), p. 56
26. Mark 15:34. The opening words of Psalm 22
27. *The Rays and the Initiations*, Alice A. Bailey, (Lucis Press, 1960), pp. 695, 524
28. Same as ref. 16, p. 279

9: The Purpose of Human Life III

And a certain ruler asked him, saying, Good Master, what shall I do to inherit eternal life? And Jesus said unto him, Why callest thou me good? None is good, save one, that is, God.[1]

Luke

God is spirit; and those who worship him must worship in spirit and in truth.[2]

John

Yet know that he who deems to conceive of God in the plenitude of his nature is guilty of presumption, for it is as impossible for a man to conceive of God as for the ant on its anthill to conceive of man. Nevertheless did Jesus call God the Father; yet is He more than the Father; and God is love, yet is He more than love – nay, God is all that it is possible to conceive of, yet is He more than is possible to conceive of.[3]

Vision of the Nazarene

Perfection is not a static condition. When the ONE of which you are a part manifests, it is in order to add to the perfection. Perfection is fulfilment to the degree that this is possible in a certain stage of development.[4]

Gita Keiller

We shall begin this chapter by noting certain features of the human body and then considering it as an allegory.[5] From one point of view the human body consists of millions upon millions of cells. They are of many different kinds and have many different functions. But all are conscious, i.e. have the capacity to be aware and to respond, though they are not, of course, self-conscious. In some strange way there is within the human body a hierarchy of beings. Few cells function

133

independently, nearly all function as one of a small (relative to the totality of cells) group, for example to form a muscle. Nor are most small groups independent. In conjunction with other small groups they function as part of a larger group, for example the heart. Proceeding in this way we eventually arrive at the (human and self-conscious) being whose consciousness informs the entire body. About this picture there are several points of interest.

(1)   Until we arrive at the (human and self-conscious) being whose consciousness informs the whole body, all lesser beings are part of something greater than themselves.

(2)   Harmony prevails, i.e. the body functions as it is intended to function, if every being in the body, whether humble like the cell or exalted like the heart, fulfils its responsibilities, i.e. performs effficiently its rightful function, and is afforded its rights, i.e. the conditions under which it can perform efficiently its rightful function.

(3)   Disharmony occurs when some being in the body no longer fulfils its responsibilities, with the result that the body no longer functions as it should. An obvious example is cancer. In colloquial terms the cancer cells kick over the traces and embark on a policy of ruthless self-aggrandisement. In due course this leads to either the destruction of the cells concerned, together probably with a host of 'innocent' cells as well, or to a condition in which the body can no longer function and there is death.

Genesis 1:27 states 'God created man in his own image, in the image of God created he him; male and female created he them.' And we are doubtless familiar with the quip that man has returned the compliment by creating God in the image of man. That there is grave danger here there is no doubt. But if the danger is kept firmly in mind, the statement in Genesis is suggestive. The retort by Jesus recorded in Luke 19:18 is also noteworthy: 'Why callest thou me good? None is good, save one, that is, God.' These two quotations prompt three questions, asked in all humility:

THE PURPOSE OF HUMAN LIFE III

(i)   To whom is the Christ responsible? Who is 'the Father' referred to in Chap. 14 to 17 of St John's Gospel, and of whom St Luke records 'Father, if thou be willing remove this cup from me: nevertheless not my will, but thine be done?'

(ii)   Who is 'the One in whom we live and move and have our being?'

(iii)   Are there no intermediaries between on the one hand, the Lord of the World, the God of this planet; and, on the other, humanity? Is there no reality behind such phrases as 'The Inner Government of the World', 'The Hierarchy of Masters', 'The Communion of Saints', 'Angels and Archangels and all the Company of Heaven'?

Without making any attempt to provide an explicit answer to these questions, what follows is put forward as a suggestion: that humanity stands in a comparable relationship to the Lord of the World, the informing consciousness of this planet – as the cells in a human body do to a human being, the informing consciousness of the body.[6] In this analogy the Christ would correspond to the heart. Such a concept enables tentative answers to be given to the above questions and is not inconsistent with the quotation from Genesis.

In *The Candle of Vision* A.E. writes:

> There came through meditation a more powerful orientation of my being as if to a hidden sun, and my thoughts turned more and more to the spiritual life of Earth. I felt instinctively that all I saw in vision was part of the Life of Earth which is a court where there are many starry palaces. There the Planetary Spirit was King, and that Spirit manifesting through the substance of Earth, the Mighty Mother, was, I felt, the being I groped after as God. The love I had for nature as garment of that deity grew deeper.[7]

Between humanity and the Lord of the World there are doubtless very many exalted beings: among them the Christ, a world Saviour, with responsibility to the Lord of the World

135

for the spiritual development of mankind. And the Buddha, the other supreme Teacher to have graced this planet during the last two and a half thousand years, what of him? We do not know, but the following extracts from *The Externalisation of the Hierarchy* and *The Unfinished Autobiography of Alice Bailey* are pointers.

There is an increasing emphasis being given in the West by esotericists to the Full Moon of May, which is the Festival of the Buddha and is held at the time when He makes His annual contact with humanity. There have been two main reasons why this effort has been made. One was the desire on the part of the Hierarchy to bring to the attention of the public the fact of the two Avatars, the Buddha and the Christ, who were the first of our humanity to come forth as human-divine Avatars and to embody in Themselves certain Cosmic Principles and give them form. The Buddha embodied the Principle of Light, and because of this illumination, humanity was enabled to recognise Christ, Who embodied the still greater Principle of Love. The second reason was to initiate the theme of the new world religion. This theme will eventually underlie all religious observances, colour all approaches to the divine centre of spiritual life, give the clue to all healing processes, and – using light scientifically – govern all techniques for bringing about conscious unity and relationship between a man and his soul, and between humanity and the Hierarchy.[8]

I twice, whilst living and working in Great Britain, took part in an extraordinary ceremony and it was nearly two decades after my participation that I discovered what it was all about. The ceremony in which I took part, I eventually found out, takes place every year at the time of the 'Full Moon of May'. I found myself whilst wide awake, in a Himalayan valley. [This ceremony presumably takes place at the etheric level and so would not be apparent to normal vision.] The people in the valley faced towards a narrow, bottle-necked passage at the end. Just before this funnel shaped passage there stood an immense rock, rising out of the floor of the valley like a great table. Standing ahead of the crowd and in front of the rock were three Figures. They formed a triangle and, to my surprise, the one at the apex of the triangle seemed to me to be the Christ. Suddenly, the three Figures before the rock stretched out Their arms towards the heavens. At the far end of the bottle-neck a Figure was seen in the sky, hovering over the passage and slowly approaching the rock. I knew in some subjective and certain fashion that it was the Buddha. I knew at the same time that in no way was our Christ belittled. I got a glimpse of the unity and the Plan to which the Christ, the Buddha and all the Masters are eternally dedicated. I realised for the first time, though in a dim and uncertain manner, the unity of all manifestation and that all existence – the material world, the spiritual realm, the aspiring disciple, the evolving animal and the beauty of the vegetable and mineral kingdoms – constituted one divine and living whole. I grasped – faintly – that human beings needed the Christ and the Buddha and all the Members of the planetary Hierarchy.[9]

In relation to question (ii) – 'Who is the One in whom we live and move and have our being?' The answer surely is 'The Lord of the World, the informing consciousness of this planet.' But just as the cells in a human body can frustrate the functioning of that body and its informing consciousness, so can humanity frustrate the plans and purposes of the Lord of the World. Some remarks made recently by the Teacher referred to in Chapters 7 and 8 are very apposite.

These next few years will determine whether this becomes a dead planet and the great power of creation is, as it were, blocked on this planet. In the great galaxy of planets this has happened before many times, and they are left as dead planets, planets without life yet where life has been. Let not this happen to this most beautiful planet of earth. Pray that it may become the garden it was meant to be, and was created as such. Pray that those living in it may learn to live in harmony both with each other and with the animals and the creatures and with their own soil, their own plants, their own trees, their own surroundings. For man has forgotten that all this is of the Spirit, every atom, all is one. Only when man is in harmony and love with his fellow men, will the lion lie down with the lamb. Only when he ceases to take with greed from the animals who serve

137

him and from the very soil on which he lives. Only when he has learned that, will he know how to live. That my friends, is the beginning of the New Age which should come upon this earth and open up the light of the spirit: but only if the majority of mankind turns towards the centre, as prodigal sons back to the Father.

A question which inevitably crops up now is 'Is the Lord of the World supreme, or is there one yet greater than he to whom the Lord of the World is responsible?' Although such a question, and any answer, however tentative, is in the realm of speculation, it is interesting to note references to the Solar Logos in sundry occult books. If such a being is accepted as a possibility, a very ancient prayer, the Gayatri in the *Rig-Veda*, assumes added significance:

> O thou who givest sustenance to the universe
> From whom all things proceed
> To whom all things return,
> Unveil to us the face of the true Spiritual Sun
> Hidden by a disc of golden light
> That we may know the Truth
> And do our whole duty
> As we journey to Thy Sacred Feet.

From this it would appear that any being, however exalted, is part of a yet greater being. But the consciousness of such beings, and of those who work with them is at levels of awareness of which no human being, no matter how exalted, can be aware in any way whatever. To speculate further is therefore pointless. What matters today is that the members of the human family should take to heart the Buddha's injunction 'work out your own salvation with diligence', i.e. strive towards the consciousness achieved by the Buddha and the Christ.

To the question, 'Has any being achieved perfection?' the answer would seem to be, 'In relation to what has been experienced and left behind, yes. To what is being experienced or has yet to be experienced, no.' Life, manifest, is ever-becoming.

We must now consider a concept to which reference so far has been only implicit – 'The Christian Trinity', especially in relation to what meaning can be given to 'The Second Person of the Trinity'. The writer is well aware of the saying 'Fools rush in where angels fear to tread', and realises that the Christian Trinity is a concept about which the saying may be singularly apt in view of the violence of past controversy. But current confusion is such that in the interests of the sincere seeker, the asking of one or two leading questions is inescapable. Whether these questions can be answered is another matter.

The first question, asked in all reverence, is 'Is the Christ, the Head of the Hierarchy, to be identified as the Second Person of the Christian Trinity?' The second question is 'What is the One, of which the Three Persons of the Christian Trinity are aspects? Is it the Lord of the World, the informing consciousness of this planet; the Solar Logos, the informing consciousness of the solar system; or One yet greater. Which of these is God?'

The mere asking of these two questions is sufficient to demonstrate the prevailing confusion, and to show the impossibility of providing anything but the most tentative of answers.

In some way which far transcends human comprehension, it does appear that the first, second, and third Persons or Aspects are associated with will, consciousness *per se*, and creation, respectively. And that this association exists at all levels, i.e. for the Lord of the World, the Solar Logos, and beyond. In the case of the Lord of the World, the God of this planet, the quality of consciousness which is of supreme importance is love, cf. 1 John, 4:8, 'He that loveth not knoweth not God; for God is love.' And of this quality Christ was the supreme exemplar. What light does this throw on the first of our two questions? It indicates that Christ, though not the second aspect of the Lord of the World, is a living symbol of that aspect. Two thousand years ago in Palestine, He manifested as much of the second aspect of the Lord of the World as was possible within the extreme limitations of the physical body. Moreover, as World Saviour, responsible to the Lord of the World for the spiritual development of mankind, it is probable that he was able to act as a channel – and still does – for energies which had never before been able to reach the human race. Failure to distinguish between (i) Jesus, the Initiate; (ii) Christ, World Saviour and Head of the Hierarchy; and (iii) the Cosmic Christ, the second 'Person' of the Christian Trinity, the love-wisdom aspect of the Lord of the World, has led to great confusion.

Now what of the second question – 'Who is the Being we refer to as God?' The answer to this, in so far as an answer is possible or meaningful, is that it is partly a matter of definition. For humanity, God is the Lord of the World, the informing consciousness of this planet in whom in very truth we live, and move, and have our being. But it is well to remember that this planet is part of a much larger scheme which has for its God the Solar Logos. This last point is important as it means that humanity is not responsible for itself alone, but has responsibilities which extend far beyond this planet.

Finally, a word of warning. In many religions there are Trinities, for example, Isis, Osiris, Horus, in the religion of ancient Egypt; Siva, Vishnu, Brahma, in Hinduism. That there are certain parallels between these Trinities, including the Christian Trinity, is clear. But to equate them is dangerous, and can lead to confusion.

A fitting end to this Chapter are some further remarks by the Teacher referred to on page 121.

> Picture a great globe of light, the centre of all creation, the alpha, the beginning – God (as you understand). This was the beginning of evolution. Progress must be outward and onward from that golden centre of all knowledge, all power, all love, all beauty. Mankind had to leave the centre and go forth in order to return. This is the pattern, and for that pattern man was subject to immutable laws. The law of cause and effect was one

that could not, and never will, be changed. In his progress outward he was to evolve into the different levels of consciousness. On the outward path he was to develop a mind, emotions, personality, gifts (if you call them such), arts, crafts, reason. All this man had to develop on his outward journey to become an individual. As your Bible has so beautfully phrased it, he was exiled from the Garden of Eden. He left the Garden of Eden which was the power, and the beauty, and the oneness with the great creative Spirit. This was and ever will be the path of man's progress to perfection. He had to develop himself and all that he was and could be, before he could become the perfect man. The only way in which this could be done was for man himself to turn outwards and to experience. So man through ages upon ages has suffered and found himself, and lost himself and found himself again. All the time he has been working outwards towards the perimeter of a great circle of evolution. Yet in this great pilgrimage outwards man began to forget the inner power of the Godhead. He became too much at one with the material world which he himself, as it were, created by his thought, and by his actions causing, sadly, troubles, fears, wars. Having reached the perimeter man must now begin to turn back towards the path. This is truly the return of the prodigal son. He has gone forth from his Father's house; he has forgotten his Father's words; he has lost the oneness with his Father, the great creative spirit of beauty, love and wisdom. Now he has come to the moment in evolution, which has taken thousands even millions of your years, when he must turn back, or this experiment will die. Yet the creative force which is in every man will not allow this wonderful experiment to die. Your planet, which is part of a greater (far far greater) scheme, has come to the point of no return. Mankind cannot go on without God or without the oneness of the great spirit of life, and that is what so much of humanity is trying to do. But in his evolution outwards man has progressed to a very high degree; he has created beauty on this earth; he has created music that is beautiful; he has found love and service.

From the time when man became a person with his own powers of thought and reasoning, lines of advance were laid down, so that men were gradually gathered into varying lines of progress. The group souls, which at that time were much larger

141

than now, were aligned to form smaller groups that were progressing along the same lines of progress. Teachers, priests, rulers, artists, musicians, sculptors, are being brought forward incarnation after incarnation so that with each life they become more at one with their own line of progress. They advance in their own way, they become at last masters of their art. This is all good, it is part of the divine light and law. It makes a glorious pattern of life.

The attraction of glamour, the blindness of selfishness, have brought the troubles which are now upon this planet. In the great law of cause and effect, the effect is now being shown, the effect of drawing away from the spirit of all life. This trauma cannot be stopped; it is an immutable law which has been working, and is working out to its uttermost. You cannot turn people back, you cannot make them return; but you can do much to influence the climate of men's minds and thought, to show them in a gentle way the cause and effect which has brought them at this moment to supreme danger. The church has taught, religions have taught, but they have failed. Man has to find himself by his own thought, by his own sufferings, his own realisations. He will have to say 'I will arise and go to my Father.'

There are many many groups in the western world, and in the eastern world, which are trying to return to the Spirit. These groups, working with the Spirit, can save this experiment of humanity. Man has now to turn back to learn a greater development of the Spirit and the immutable laws of the Spirit. God's will is perfection, and only by returning to the centre with the advanced minds men have attained will they eventually, in many thousands of years, attain perfection. Such is the divine progress. From the centre to the periphery beautifully developing individuality, then returning with all that has accrued, towards perfection.

Five propositions are suggested by the matters discussed in this chapter.

(1) The Lord of the World, the name given to the informing consciousness of this planet, is the God in whom in very truth we live, and move, and have our being.

(2)   The relationship between the Lord of the World and humanity is analogous to the relationship between a human being and the cells in his/her body.

(3)   Christ, as Head of the Hierarchy, is the link between the Lord of the World and humanity, and is responsible to the Lord of the World for humanity's spiritual development.

(4)   Christ is the dynamic symbol of the second aspect of the Lord of the World, i.e. of the Second Person of the Christian Trinity, sometimes referred to as the Cosmic Christ. Two thousand years ago in Palestine He manifested as much of the second aspect of the Lord of the World as was possible within the extreme limitations of the physical body.

(5)   Beyond the Lord of the World is the Solar Logos; beyond the Solar Logos is the 'One about whom naught may be said'. Not because it is forbidden, but becuse about such a Being nothing meaningful can be expressed in words.

References

1.   Luke 18:18
2.   John 4:24
3.   *The Vision of the Nazarene*, by the author of *The Initiate*, (Neville Spearman, 1955), p. 25
4.   *Let Life Live*, Gita Keiller, (The Mitre Press, 1975), p. 9
5.   cf. 1 Corinthians 12:12–27
6.   cf. Teilhard de Chardin's approach on pp. 251 and 262 of *The Phenomenon of Man*, (Collins, 1959)
7.   *The Candle of Vision*, A.E., (Macmillan, 1918), p. 29
8.   *The Externalisation of the Hierarchy*, Alice A. Bailey, (Lucis Press, 1958), p. 347
9.   *The Unfinished Autobiography of Alice Bailey*, (Lucis Press, 1951), p. 38

10: The Potentialities of the Ordinary Man or Woman

Know thyself, and thou wilt know the Universe and the Gods.

Inscription on the Temple of Delphi

The Self can be defined as an inner guiding factor that is different from the conscious personality . . . Investigation of one's dreams shows it to be the regulating centre that brings about a constant extension and maturing of the personality . . . How far it develops depends on whether the ego is willing to listen to the messages of the Self.[1]

Carl Jung

. . . to whom God was pleased to make known this mystery . . . which is Christ in you, the hope of glory.[2]

Colossians 1:27

The supreme purpose of God is birth. He will not be content until his Son is born in us. Neither will the soul be content until the Son is born of it.[3]

Meister Eckhart

So long as man clamours for the *I* and the *Mine*
    his works are as naught:
When all love of the *I* and the *Mine* is dead,
    then the work of the Lord is done.[4]

Kabir

In the three preceding chapters we have considered the first of the two fundamental questions raised in Chapter 1 – 'What is the purpose of human life on this planet?' It is now time to consider the second fundamental question – 'What are the potentialities of the ordinary man or woman?' At the end of each of the last four chapters the writer has listed a number of propositions which in his opinion are indicated – not, be it emphasised, proved – by the evidence and subsequent discussion. Of these propositions, those which have a direct bearing on the subject matter of this chapter are the following:

(i)   Man is triple: personality, soul (or Higher Self), and spirit (the monad or atman).

(ii)   Man evolves through a series of physical lives, the circumstances of which are interconnected.

(iii)   The fruits of each incarnation, i.e. the qualities developed and the skills acquired, are absorbed by the soul.

(iv)   The soul remembers the past, is in touch with the future, and is itself evolving.

(v)   As the soul evolves the link between soul and personality grows stronger.

(vi)   There are many levels of consciousness, and many grades of matter.

(vii)   Human life has a purpose – the expansion and intensification of consciousness – without limit. Expressed a little differently, the destiny of man on this planet is to be able to perform in the drama of life whatever part he is called upon to play with grace, skill and selfless dedication, i.e. to become a master of the art and science of living.

When considering an applicant's ability to fill a vacant post, an important factor is the applicant's make-up – physical, emotional, intellectual and spiritual. When this is known some estimate of what the person may be capable becomes possible. When considering the potentialities of the ordinary man or woman similar reasoning applies. His or her constitution – physical, emotional, intellectual and spiritual – is clearly of cardinal importance. Let us see therefore if we can find a scientifically acceptable account of man's constitution. But where to look? The answer is not clear. Since once we go beyond man's purely physical structure and functioning, about which a great deal is known, understood and generally agreed, we enter a field where not much is known or understood, and little is generally agreed. Of well established schools of psychology there are a significant number, and their tenets range from those which adhere to an out and out behaviourist concept of man – the belief that eventually everything will be explicable in terms of the purely physical – to those which, while accepting the contribution made by behaviourism, maintain that in itself it is but a pale and often deceptive sign of something far more deeply interfused. Amongst the latter are many well known psychologists who hold broadly similar views on a number of fundamental principles. In an attempt to co-ordinate and synthesise the vast amount of studies and research material now available, Dr Assagioli, the founder of psychosynthesis, has 'arrived at a pluridimensional conception of the human personality' which he considers to be 'more inclusive and nearer to reality than previous formulations'. A diagrammatic representation of this conception is reproduced as Figure 4.[5]

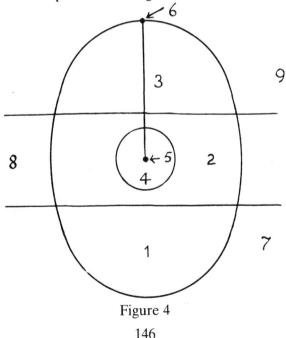

Figure 4

The notes which follow are extracts from, or summaries of, Dr Assagioli's observations.

The Lower Unconscious (1)
This contains the elementary psychological activities which direct the life of the body, the intelligent co-ordination of bodily functions; the fundamental drives and primitive urges; many complexes, charged with intense emotion; dreams and imaginations of an inferior kind; lower, uncontrolled parapsychological processes; various pathological manifestations, such as phobias, obsessions, compulsive urges and paranoid delusions.

The Middle Unconscious (2)
This is formed of psychological elements similar to those of waking consciousness and easily accessible to it. In this inner region our various experiences are assimilated, and developed before their birth into the light of consciousness.

The Higher Unconscious or Superconscious (3)
From this region we receive our higher intuitions and inspirations – artistic, philosophical or scientific. It is the source of the higher feelings, such as altruistic love; of genius and of the states of contemplation, illumination, and ecstasy. In this realm are latent the higher psychic functions and spiritual energies.

The Field of Consciousness (4)
This term is used to designate that part of our personality of which we are directly aware: the incessant flow of sensations, images, thoughts, feelings, desires, and impulses which we can observe, analyse, and judge.

The Conscious Self or 'I' (5)
This is the point of pure self-awareness, not to be confused with the conscious personality described in the preceding paragraph. The changing contents of our consciousness (the

sensations, thoughts, feelings, etc.) are one thing; the 'I', the self, the centre of our consciousness is another.

The Higher Self (6)
The higher self is above, and unaffected by, the flow of the mindstream or by bodily conditions; and the personal conscious self should be considered merely as its reflection, its 'projection' in the field of the personality. This concept is corroborated by 'such philosophers as Kant and Herbart, who make a clear distinction between the empirical ego and the noumenal or real Self.'

The Lower, Middle, and Higher Collective Unconscious (7), (8), (9)
The outer line of the oval of the diagram should be regarded as 'delimiting' but not as dividing. It should be regarded as analogous to the membrane delimiting a cell, which permits a constant and active interchange with the whole body to which the cell belongs. Processes of 'psychological osmosis' are going on all the time, both with other human beings and with the general psychic environment. The latter corresponds to what Jung has called the collective unconscious.

Comparing Assagioli's picture of man with the propositions with which this chapter started, there emerges a significant overall consistency. For although Assagioli refers to various matters not touched on by the propositions, and vice versa, the fact remains that where there is overlap the views expressed are similar. This is notably true regarding the existence of a higher self or soul, perhaps the most important single feature in this particular concept of man.

The Kahunas (literally, 'Keepers of the Secret') of Polynesia regarded man as a triune being composed of a low self – the subconscious; a middle self – the conscious mind or entity; and a high self – the superconscious or Guardian Angel. As this was long before Freud or Jung, this is surprising and prompts the question – 'Whence came such knowledge?' In *The Secret Science at Work*, Max Freedom Long points out that 'In the totem pole of the North American natives there is a central column made up of one figure set directly above another . . . Still higher up, and seldom so closely united, comes a figure which often has spreading wings, and which is ideal as a representation of the Guardian Angel or High Self.'[6]

The orthodox Christian view – 1 Thessalonians 5:23 – is that man is 'body, soul and spirit', though the extent to which soul in this context has the same meaning as higher self (as used in this chapter) is doubtful. But what is not in doubt is the assertion that behind man's personality consciousness lies something which is both deeper and nobler. And the same is profoundly true of the basic affirmation of Indian metaphysics *Tat Tvam Asi* – THAT thou art.

Of immediate relevance to our theme is the following passage from *The Flame and the Light* by H. l'A. Fausset.

> As we begin to be conscious of ourselves and of the nature of the world in which we move, we seem to divide inwardly into two beings. These two beings the *Mundaka Upanishad* describes as 'two birds, close friends, who dwell on the same tree'. One eats the fruit of the tree, the other looks on in silence. The first is the human self, who, though active, is bewildered and sad. 'But when he sees that other, his Lord and beloved, his sorrow passes away.' Ultimately this is so. But it is long before the distracted eater of the fruit of the tree of life knows his other self to be his friend.
>
> In each of us, the Masters teach, a fully conscious and undeluded being waits to be known. In that realization we shall be reconciled with ourselves and also with life. We shall no longer be subject to blind alternations of attraction and repulsion as we grasp at the fruit of life. For we shall contemplate life truly and lovingly in the act of living it.[7]

From what was touched on in Chapters 7 to 9 and has been emphasised in the last few pages, it follows that the problem which confronts the ordinary man and woman at this time is how to construct a bridge between the personality and the soul (or Higher Self); in terms used by Assagioli, how to establish a link between 'the empirical ego and the real Self'. *À propos* of Figure 1 in Chapter 8 the task is to surmount the barrier BB. In Chapter 6 it was pointed out that whatever lives can be studied from the standpoint of form or from the standpoint of consciousness. In Chapter 8 it was suggested that the kind of thoughts and feelings which we habitually harbour will affect the mental and emotional matter in our 'body', and that the quality of the mental and emotional matter in our 'body' will condition our thoughts and feelings. If this is correct, it follows that we can consider the desired-for bridge between personality and soul either from the standpoint of form or from the standpoint of consciousness. In the rest of this chapter we shall adopt each standpoint in turn.

There is a long tradition, backed by no little evidence, that permeating man's physical body, and extending a little beyond it, is some kind of field. The names most commonly used to describe this field are health aura, etheric field, etheric body, body of vitality.[8] Though not yet recognised by science, the etheric field is said to be an integral part of our physical space-time world, and can be seen with the physical eyes by those who have developed etheric vision (not to be confused with those, many more in number, who claim to 'see' – but not with the physical eyes – man's emotional-mental body, loosely referred to as 'the aura'). In *Esoteric Psychology* it is stated: 'This is physiological and not a psychic power and is quite different to clairvoyance. There can be no etheric vision apart from the usual organ of vision, the eye.'[9] And in *Frontiers of Revelation*, Frances Banks says:

> It was in the chapel after Vespers one evening that I had my first experience of etheric vision. I saw my companion as she stood, walked, sat and knelt – changed, as it were, into a thick, creamy, highly vibratory substance, interpenetrating through and beyond the body and the thick covering of a heavy overcoat,

yet retaining their contours. Blink, move or re-examine as I would, the effect remained the same; a physical seeing, shorn of any vestige of imagination. Shortly afterwards I was to see the etheric in other people, whether patchy-grey or a glowing cream; also trees, flowers, and a whole bank of geraniums, all dissolving, as it seemed, into etheric substance. But nothing was ever again so startling and convincing a proof that normal vision (with perhaps a slightly different focus) could register the fact of a finer and more volatile substance interpenetrating the dense physical substance ordinarily seen. There was, I would emphasize, no hint of what is called 'clairvoyance', in which another image is superimposed upon the prevailing physical environment.[10]

The etheric field is said to act as a matrix for the physical body, and its condition is apparently both crucial and revealing in respect of a person's physical, emotional, mental and spiritual condition. Unfortunately, or maybe fortunately having regard to mankind's present state of spiritual development, the number of people who have etheric vision is very small. One such was the late Mrs Bendit (*née* Phoebe Payne) who was a close friend of the writer and whose books on the subject under discussion are of considerable interest. What follows are three extracts.

General ill-health shows in the vital field as a whole, but local disease produces marked local changes as well as a disturbance of the whole. Thus a superficial cut or bruise is visible etherically as well as physically. There is a slight break in the rhythm of the vital currents over the site of the injury. Such things as malignant disease or abscess formation show both a generally deranged etheric field and a localized condition. This is often visible long before there is any evidence of organic trouble. It begins as a patch of disorganization of the currents in the particular part of the field over the organ affected. The rhythmic flow becomes broken and irregular, and small vortices form in which, as in a river whirlpool, waste matter accumulates instead of being thrown out. The natural colour disappears, and the whole texture becomes denser as the waste material coagulates, just as mud is deposited by water. The movement slows down until real stagnation occurs. Then, at a certain point, the whole process becomes as it were precipitated into the level of the physical tissues and local organic disease is established.

Thought and feeling, not to mention profounder spiritual activity, are constantly reflected into the health aura, which changes from moment to moment as mental processes take place. There is an Indian saying that 'Prana [vitality][11] follows thought'. This is indeed seen to be a fact because there is an immediate alteration in the health aura as mood and thinking change.[12]

On the surface of the etheric field or body are seven force centres.

Each of these psychic organs, looked at clairvoyantly [used here to include *all* non-normal vision] is described as roughly in the shape of a cornucopia, with its narrow end based at a critical point in the physical spinal cord, and its mouth extending to the edge of the etheric aura . . . The cornucopia shape is due not to a fixed structure but to the play of two streams of psychic energy weaving together. One of these, flowing in the spinal cord, is thrown out from the centre and flows towards the periphery in a widening spiral; this represents the motor stream. The second stream, impinging on the surface of the etheric body, spirals inward, narrowing as it goes; this is the receptive or sensory stream. These two spirals flow parallel to one another, but in opposite directions, and may be compared to interlocking screw-threads, in that one may be said to run in the grooves of the other. They give an impression of spinning, like the fluid in the vortex of a whirlpool. It is this characteristic rotary movement which gives these centres their Sanskrit name of 'chakras' or wheels.[13]

The chakras, or force centres, are of paramount functional importance, as they are in effect the organs by which psycho-spiritual man expresses himself in the etheric, and thence in the dense physical world. Taken collectively, they should be a balanced system, each one of which reflects a certain form of psychic activity; while taken together they are a manifestation of the whole of the individual in action. Nothing of non-physical

152

man becomes effective in the dense worlds except through the chakras.[14]

Of these centres, four – the head centre, the Ajna centre (between the eye brows; sometimes referred to as the third eye), the throat centre, and the heart centre – are above the diaphragm; three – the solarplexus centre, the sacral centre, and the centre at the base of the spine – are below the diaphragm. As evolution proceeds there is a steady transfer of energies from the centres below the diaphragm, first to the heart and throat centres, and then to the Ajna and head centres. 'The energy at the base of the spine has to be transferred to the head; the energy of the sacral centre must be lifted to the throat, whilst the energy of the solarplexus must be transferred to the heart.'[15] For most of mankind the Ajna and head centres are not very active. It seems likely that it was to the functioning of the Ajna centre that Jesus was referring when he said: 'If therefore thine eye be single, thy whole body shall be full of light.' The head centre is the last centre to awake and is said only to become fully active towards the end of the human journey. Tradition has it that the Ajna centre is 'the throne of the soul', and that the head centre, sometimes referred to as the thousand petalled lotus – in another tradition the Holy Grail, the Chalice of Love, ready to receive the Wine of the Spirit – provides the link with the monad. Regarded from the standpoint of form, the problem is to construct a bridge of which the first span to be built goes from the heart centre via the throat centre to the Ajna centre, and the second span goes from the Ajna centre to the head centre. When constructed, this bridge will span what for most people is the gap in consciousness between personality, soul and monad, and will thus provide the way along which the centre of consciousness can move at will to any of the levels of consciousness shown diagrammatically in Figure 2 on p. 115. In the literature this way or path is referred to as the antahkarana or rainbow bridge. Constructing the antahkarana and waking the relevant centres is said to come

153

about quite naturally as a result of steady and persistent effort to shift the centre of consciousness away from the desires and aversions of the personality towards concern for the well-being of the group, the well-being of the whole. As preoccupation with likes and dislikes by the empirical self becomes less intense, it becomes possible for the still small voice of the higher self or soul to make itself heard. When this channel of communication, this 'way of familiar approach', has become sufficiently well established, we have what has been previously referred to as a soul-infused personality. In the Christian tradition this is sometimes referred to as 'the birth of the Christ within the heart', cf. the third and fourth quotations at the beginning of this chapter. And this is a goal, though not in any sense an ultimate or final goal, which is due to be achieved – albeit perhaps only after many lives – by all members of the human family.

Reconciling the duality presented by the personality consciousness and the higher self or soul with the concept of an underlying unity presents a very real problem. But the following allegory may prove helpful.

Consider someone whom we will refer to as X and who is teaching himself (or, of course, herself) to type. In the early stages, locating and touching the right keys demands X's complete attention; there is nothing left over for considering the sense of what is being typed. At this stage almost everyone finds that some key or sequence of keys proves difficult, and has to take extra care and time to overcome the difficulty. With practice the process becomes less laboured, and in time the stage is reached when X can type with relative fluency and ease something already written. At this stage X may have a hazy idea about the meaning of what he is typing, but at best it will be no more than hazy. If X starts to think about the meaning of what he is typing, his actual typing will go to pieces. After a lot more practice comes X's ability to compose a talk and to type it at the same time.

In this allegory X's consciousness when typing corresponds

THE POTENTIALITIES OF THE ORDINARY MAN OR WOMAN

to his personal consciousness, the consciousness of the empirical self. X's consciousness when he is reflecting on the subject about which he is intending to write corresponds to the consciousness of the higher self or soul. To begin with there is duality, the personal consciousness is totally unaware of the higher self or soul. When the intermediate stage is reached, i.e. of being able to type with relative fluency and ease something already written, the personal consciousness is that of a well integrated personality and is occasionally illumined by a shaft of light from the soul. When the final stage is reached, the personal consciousness is subsumed in that of the soul. 'The lighted way' has come into being. There is no longer duality.

It would seem that most of us are somewhere between the beginning and intermediate stage, and that those who have progressed beyond the intermediate stage are very few.

Five propositions are suggested by matters discussed in this chapter.

(1)   Permeating man's physical body and extending a little beyond it is an etheric field.

(2)   Associated with this field are seven force centres or chakras.

(3)   The condition of these centres plays an immensely important part in relation to a person's health, both physical and psychological.

(4)   Accompanying, and as a result of, a person's overall development, a 'bridge' starts to be built, first between the heart centre via the throat centre to the Ajna centre, and then between the Ajna centre and the head centre.

(5)   Following the construction of this 'bridge' – the rainbow bridge or antahkarana – there comes into being a soul-infused personality.

References

1.   *Man and his Symbols*, conceived and edited by Carl Jung, (Aldus Books, 1964), Chap. 3, 'The Process of Individuation' by M-L von Franz, p. 162

2. Colossians 1:27
3. *Meister Eckhart*, translation by Raymond B. Blakney, (Harper & Row, New York, 1941), Sermon 12, p. 151
4. *Kabir's Poems*, translated by Rabindranath Tagore, p. 5
5. *Psychosynthesis*, Roberto Assagioli, (Hobbs, Dorman & Co., New York, 1965), p. 17
6. *The Secret Science at Work*, Max Freedom Long, (Huna Research Publications, Vista, California, 1953), p. 72
7. *The Flame and the Light*, H. l'A. Fausset, (Abelard-Schuman, 1958), p. 28
8. See *Breakthrough to Creativity*, Shafica Karagulla, (DeVorss & Co., Santa Monica, U.S.A., 1967)
9. *A Treatise on the Seven Rays*, Alice A. Bailey, Vol. 2, 'Esoteric Psychology', (Lucis Press, 1942), p. 608
10. *Frontiers of Revelation*, Frances Banks, (Max Parrish, London, 1962), p. 27
11. See *A Treatise on Cosmic Fire*, Alice A. Bailey, (Lucis Press, 1952. First published 1925)
12. *Man Incarnate*, P. D. Bendit and Laurence Bendit, (Theosophical Publishing House, 1957), pp. 19, 23
13. *The Psychic Sense*, P. D. Payne and L. J. Bendit, (Faber & Faber, 1958), p. 97
14. Same as ref. 12, p. 25
15. *Esoteric Healing*, Alice A. Bailey, (Lucis Press, 1953), p. 138

Part IV
Application

11: Guide Lines

Information is not knowledge, but a means whereby knowledge may be acquired. Knowledge is not wisdom, but has been called the ladder to wisdom, and wisdom is the goal of the disciple.

The ladder of knowledge does not stand ready prepared and erected for the use of the learner: he has to fashion it himself with pain and labour, and experience is the material with which he builds. Facts and ideas that come to him from his teacher, though knowledge to the teacher, are not so to him: they are specialized fields of experience which only become knowledge if diligently explored and the results assimilated.[1]

P. G. Bowen

Three things come not back; the spent arrow, the spoken word, and the lost opportunity.

Arab Proverb

It is, unfortunately, only too clear that if the individual is not truly regenerated in spirit, society cannot be either, for society is the sum total of individuals in need of redemption.[2]

C. G. Jung

It is bridging work which has now to be done – bridging between what is today and what can be in the future. If, during the next 150 years, we develop this technique of bridging the many cleavages found in the human family and in offsetting the racial hatred and the separative attitudes of nations and people, we shall have succeeded in implementing a world in which war will be impossible and humanity will be realizing itself as one human family and not as a fighting aggregate of many nations and people, competitively engaged in getting the best of each other and successfully fostering prejudices and hatred.[3]

Djwhal Khul

> We shall have to repent in this generation, not so much for the evil deeds of the wicked people, but for the appalling silence of the good people.
>
> Martin Luther King

'Thought without action is arid. Action without thought is chaos.' Taoist thought also considers *appropriate* inaction to be action. It is an *inner* action taken to forestall a wrong *external* action. An example is, when appropriate, minding one's own business and not interfering.

The starting point is to realise that for creative living, thought and action are a team, and that thought which does not lead to action turns sour. Moreover, we have to start from where, and what, we are. Not, as in the story of the Cockney who, when asked the way, replied 'If I were you, I wouldn't start from 'ere!'

What follows is an extract from a letter sent to P. G. Bowen by his Teacher in response to an enquiry.

If I were called upon to give the best advice I could to a beginner who I had reason to suppose was in real earnest, I think it would be somewhat as follows: 'Using ordinary commonsense and discretion, take some teaching that comes from a source that sounds pure and rings reasonably true: *take it as a working hypothesis and try honestly to live it out*. In the process which must enter into the daily details of life, avoid quixotism, or over-concern with self; do and leave – even in thought. Work, watch and do your best to wake up your intuition and recognize its voice amid the chatter of the lower mentality. Keep the head from being over busy; put intellectual modes and standards at less value than most of your contemporaries, and do not regard them as final arbiters.'

The trouble is that most students will do any blessed thing rather than that indicated in the italicized passage. I saw a really excellent little parable the other day: 'Wanted for the building of (the New) Jerusalem, fewer architects and more bricklayers', and I recommend it as advice to those you may be trying to help. Nearly all look in the wrong direction. Unless some phenomenon occurs, or some knowledge of the formulated kind expected by the Western mind enters the brain, they lose

160

faith and start looking for some other theory or movement. No teacher can give it out so that all and sundry can understand; the effort and the (for want of a better word) experiments to awaken the real sense of truth and light, are the first part of the job and cannot be done for anybody, by anybody. The student has to take the first steps unaided, not because of any reluctance on the part of older brothers to teach, but for the reason that the effort must be self-instigated.

Until perception and the wider knowledge dawn, all efforts towards power are dangerous and may be disastrous. How many, impelled by motives seeming quite good to them, have sought, and sometimes even gained and used power to further some idea of progress, some forced modification of the people or circumstances around them. Did they know even a little of the working out in time of the causes they seek to launch, they would shrink from the responsibility involved. The Kingdom must be sought first; the use of power without wisdom (not worthy sentiments) may be serious. It is infinitely more important to love our neighbour as ourselves (in the fullest meaning of the phrase) than to have the power to influence him without his knowledge and consent.

The (wider) knowledge dawns within you as you make the conditions and let go the personal thoughts and things; it's easy to some and hard to others. Let the student turn away from theory and from 'practices' to *practice*. Let him find his chief happiness in that of others, his 'power' in disentangling himself from lust and fear and greed, his knowledge in the myriad changes and cycles of Nature, and in listening to the occasional whisper of the 'still small voice'. We usually do too much instead of too little, especially with the brain-mind. The student should read less and rest more in the deeper parts of consciousness that arise when the head is not so busy; books, useful as some of them are, can often act as drugs to lull and stupefy and prevent real thinking.

In the study of any real Scripture or book on true occultism [H. P. Blavatsky defined occultism as 'The science of life, the art of living', and this is the meaning assumed here] something real will emerge if students can be induced to approach the book, not as though it were the words of someone endeavouring to force upon them his own particular ideas, *but*

161

with the single aim of discovering exactly what it does teach. This is the real key. Honest intelligent human beings, will easily recognise that it is necessary to know what a teaching really is before one can either accept or reject it. To go ahead (as most students do) objecting, criticising, perhaps even agreeing, with every passage means the worst confusion.

We will now consider in some detail a number of the points raised in this penetrating and thought-provoking letter.

(a) 'Take some teaching that comes from a source that sounds pure and rings reasonably true: *take it as a working hypothesis and try honestly to live it out.*'

Before setting out to climb a mountain peak, it is only sensible to make due and proper preparations. Not to do so is manifestly foolish. But after a while the stage is reached when all reasonable preparations have been completed, and it is time to begin the actual climb. For no matter how thorough or protracted the preparations, there can never be proof in advance that the climb will be successful. The only proof there is is to reach the summit.

And so it is with the psychological climb up 'the mount of illumination'. To make reasonable preparations is wise; to make inordinate preparations – first this teacher, then that teacher; now this book, then that book – is not. Indeed, the effect is debilitating as it undermines the will. For this climb there is no alternative to making a decision on the best evidence available, and then setting forth, with hope and with determination.

(b) 'Avoid quixotism, or over-concern with self.'

After the injunction never to part company with common sense, this sentence refers to one of the great spiritual paradoxes, pinpointed so clearly by the sayings: 'Work out your own salvation, with diligence' – the Buddha; 'For whosoever would save his soul shall lose it' – the Christ. Inconsistent? Not at all. These sayings are different sides of the same coin. The Buddha is emphasising the importance of self-instigated effort by the personal self. The Christ is saying that the Kingdom of Heaven, essentially a state of consciousness, is not attained by merely enhancing the consciousness of the personal self with its undertone of I wish or I want, or I don't wish or I don't want, for myself. In St Luke's Gospel[4] there is this passage:

> And again he said, Whereunto shall I liken the Kingdom of God? It is like unto leaven, which a woman took and hid in three measures of meal, till it was all leavened.

When in a parable reference is made to a number, it is never by chance. Here it would appear that Jesus is referring to the permeation of the personality consciousness (sensing physically, feeling emotionally, and thinking discursively) by the consciousness of the soul.[5]

In relation to what has been said about the antahkarana or rainbow bridge, the Buddha is referring to the consciousness associated with one end of the bridge, personality consciousness, and what must be done to construct the bridge; the Christ is referring to the consciousness associated with the other end of the bridge, soul consciousness. The extent to which personality consciousness and soul consciousness are different in kind, not just in degree, is shown by the following quotations.

The first quotation is from Chapter 3 of St John's Gospel.[6]

> There was a man of the Pharisees, named Nicodemus, a ruler of the Jews: the same came to Jesus by night, and said unto him, Rabbi, we know that thou art a teacher come from God: for no man can do these miracles that thou doest, except God be with him. Jesus answered and said unto him, Verily, verily, I say unto thee, Except a man be born again, he cannot see the kingdom of God. Nicodemus saith unto him, How can a man be born when he is old? Can he enter the second time into his mother's womb, and be born? Jesus answered, Verily, verily, I say unto thee, Except a man be born of water and of the Spirit, he cannot enter the kingdom of God.

The second quotation is taken from Charles Johnston's introduction to Book VI of the *Bhagavad Gita*.[7]

In Yoga it is all a question of the twofold nature of man; that marvellous paradox of blended angel and demon. There is the twofold enigma: the Personal self on the one hand, the Supreme on the other; our wonderful, complex being embracing both.

For the follower of Yoga, the great thing is to find in his heart the dim spark of the Supreme, the beginning of the small, old Path, that leads to immortal life. Finding, within, that spark, that Path, let him give his whole heart and soul to it, forgetting all else, and no longer obeying the desire of the personal self for one or another indulgence. [This marks the Birth of the Christ within the heart – 'This mystery . . . which is Christ in you, the hope of glory.'] Then, as he watches with faithful worship, the spark of pure divine consciousness in the heart will grow; the light will gather strength, and begin to illumine the secrets of his immortality. The Supreme will begin to fill the world for him, and all things will appear to him as part and parcel of the Supreme. Such a one will be lifted above himself; his consciousness will no longer dwell wholly in the personal self, but will shine out in the spiritual realm above the personal self, revealing mysteries. And that higher realm will become for him a dwelling-place, above the waters of birth and death.

A third quotation is from *The Sayings of the Ancient One* by P. G. Bowen.[8]

At this point it should be clearly understood that the spiritual, or universal consciousness which disciples, initiates, and Masters exercise in one degree or another is not merely an extension of the personal human variety, but is of a different, and higher nature altogether. *Cultivation of personal powers and faculties, no matter how intense, will never transform personal man into the disciple.* It may, and usually does, check his progress towards the spiritual life, just as over-development of the animal nature inhibits evolution of higher human qualities in the child. This does not mean that human faculties, among which intellect is predominant, should be neglected. They are all instruments of experience, and only through experience is wisdom gained.

The learner is a spiritual babe. He is born into his new world when he becomes a learner, and, like the human infant, is initially merely sentient, but not conscious as its older inhabitants are in one degree or another. His evolution in his new life proceeds in a manner analogous to that of a child towards human individuality. His primitive spiritual sentience evolves in due course into a dim, diffused spiritual awareness which in later stages flowers into spiritual self-consciousness . . .

Just as no man can describe to another who has not seen it the miracle of the dawn of an earthly day, so can no words convey to the personal mind what waking to spiritual consciousness means. To be known it must be experienced. Nothing more can be said.

If, in the above quotation, the italicised sentence (italicised by the writer) seems strange, the following analogy may be helpful. Suppose that X decides to be a professional mathematician. He must begin by acquiring competence at elementary algebra, geometry and trigonometry. When he has done that he can start on the calculus, a very powerful and necessary tool for any professional mathematician. Though competence at elementary algebra, geometry and trigonometry is essential, it does not mean the ability to do everything that can possibly be done by means of algebra, geometry and trigonometry. If X is outstandingly good at these subjects as a result of much time and effort, so be it. But in achieving his long term aim of becoming a professional mathematician, the time thus spent would have been much better spent in mastering the calculus and thus enabling him to tackle a vast range of problems which no amount of knowledge or skill at algebra, geometry and trigonometry, could ever do.

In this analogy, algebra, geometry and trigonometry, correspond to 'personal powers and faculties'; the calculus to 'spiritual self-consciousness'.

The temptation, and it is a very real temptation, of trying to attain the kingdom of Heaven by developing the personality consciousness is illustrated by the following story (in which the temptation is resisted).

The story is of how Hercules performed his third labour

165

which was to gather the golden apples of the Hesperides, the fruit of the tree of wisdom. The sacred tree which bore these apples was guarded by three maidens, and a wily dragon with a hundred heads guarded the maidens. After several years of fruitless search. during which time Hercules underwent many trials and tribulations, he at last discovered the tree, guarded as foretold. Thrilled that his objective was now within reach, and ready and eager to attack the dragon, his attention was suddenly arrested by Atlas, staggering beneath the load of worlds upon his back, his face lined with suffering, and his eyes closed with agony. Hercules, trembling, watched and gauged the measure of the load and pain. He forgot about his search. The sacred tree and apples faded from his mind. His only thought was to aid the giant, and that without delay. Forward he rushed and eagerly removed the load, lifting it off the shoulders of his brother on to his own back, thus shouldering the burden of the worlds himself. He closed his eyes, bracing himself with effort, and lo! the load rolled off, and he stood free, and likewise Atlas.

Before him stood the giant, and in his hand he held the golden apples, offering them, with love, to Hercules. The maidens fair held still more golden apples, and pressed them likewise in his hands. The search was over.[9]

In relation to this story, Djwhal Khul makes the comment: 'Not until aspirants in the religious field, and in the church and in the many esoteric groups to which they gravitate have learnt to lose sight of their spiritual selfishness by helping to bridge the economic, religious, and political cleavages which are rending humanity at this time, will there be any rapid increase in the number of those treading the path which leads from "darkness to light, from the unreal to the real, from death to immortality".'[10]

Also relevant is the following anecdote told by the late Dr Leslie Weatherhead.

A girl, still in her teens, was in a hospital dying from tuberculosis. She was the eldest child of a poor family and, her mother having died, the burden of caring for the younger ones had fallen heavily upon her youthful shoulders. She lay back upon the pillows and her work-worn hands rested on the coverlet. A visitor who doubtless meant well said to the young patient, 'Do you love God?' The answer came, 'I don't know anything about God.' 'Why,' said the visitor, 'have you never been to church?' 'I've never had time,' said the girl. 'Do you say your prayers?' said the visitor. 'I don't know any prayers,' said the girl. 'Well, what will you do when you appear in the presence of God?' The girl replied wearily and sublimely, 'I shall show him my hands.'[11]

(c) 'Do and leave – even in thought.'

Many people waste a lot of time and energy in not doing just this. On asking why, there appear to be three main reasons.

First, a philosophic one: a failure to appreciate the purpose of experience. Experience is the food which sustains us and enables us to grow – in knowledge and in wisdom. The trouble with many people in the Western World is that they consume far more food (experience) than they can digest, and so suffer from chronic indigestion (inability to extract what is of value from what is experienced). Failing to appreciate the cause of their complaint, they search for yet more food, thinking thereby to assuage their discomfort! For such a condition the appropriate treatment is change in attitude of mind – less concentration on pleasure and the happiness which is expected to ensue, and more attention to the lessons which the situations and experience that are part and parcel of ordinary living have to teach. Such a change inevitably takes time, but if the attempt is made – using common sense and persistence – the effects can be striking. If intense frustration, for example, and the irritability that goes with it, are gradually replaced by real acceptance (of something that cannot be altered), the cause of the frustration will cease to play such a dominant role, and in place of frustration there will develop peace of mind. Moreover it sometimes happens, though not of course always, that when the lessons which a particular situation has to teach have been duly learnt, the situation itself undergoes an unforeseen change.

167

The second reason is fear. Everyone must have seen a dog who, afraid of something which is unfamiliar, prowls round it. The dog cannot summon up the courage to go closer and investigate, but nor is it able to tear itself away. In thought, most of us on occasion resemble the dog. There are some situations, certain personal relationships perhaps, about which we are uneasy or afraid, but which we neither tackle nor leave alone. In such situations it is important to realise just how much time and energy are being spent to no purpose, and then make up our mind to 'do' or 'leave', i.e. to tackle the situation or forget about it. Going on going round, like the dog, neither advancing nor retreating, wastes nervous energy and eventually undermines the will.

Finally guilt. We are all familiar with accounts of the criminal who, certainly in thought and sometimes physically, cannot tear himself away from the scene of his crime. Though we may not be criminals as defined by the law, there must be few indeed who have never done or said something of which they were subsequently ashamed. As with the criminal, there is in many of us the tendency to return in thought to 'the scene of the crime'. What then to do? For those who belong to certain of the great religious traditions, confession can be an effective solvent. For those who are not, or who are averse to confession, it may be helpful to make three points. The first two are obvious, but the third may not be. (i) Repentance, i.e. facing the fact of what we have said or done, and resolving to act differently should a comparable situation arise in the future. (ii) Making amends to the person or persons wronged, if that is possible. Often it is not. (iii) Trusting in 'the good law' – karma, the law of ethical causation – and having faith that the working of 'the good law' is such that in this or some subsequent incarnation (a) we shall find ourselves in a comparable situation – comparable, that is, as calling for those qualities of character the lack of which was the cause of our failure; and (b) we shall have the opportunity to pay our karmic debt, i.e. to make amends, either to the individual we wronged, or to some other person 'on his behalf', i.e. someone who has earned the right to receive special help.

'Do and leave – even in thought' does not of course apply to the love and affection which may be felt between two people (or even by one person if the feeling is not mutual) who may be separated by distance or by death. A flash of greeting, which need not take more than a second or two in a morning's meditation, is most important. It keeps the link alive: cf. the need for the occasional flow of blood (love) in a limb (a relationship) which has been severely injured (distance or death) and which is bound by a tourniquet (restricting conditions). Moreover, people should be pictured when we knew them at their best, not – as so often happens in the case of death – when marked by age or illness.

(d) 'Watch and do your best to wake up your intuition and recognise its voice amid the chatter of the lower mentality.'

Although Bowen's Teacher warns against reliance on practices – 'let the student turn away from theory and from "practices" to *practice*' – meditation is important provided that it is regarded as a means – in the first instance for cultivating a certain attitude of mind – and not an end in itself. One of the objects is to shift the focus of consciousness away from preoccupation with the personal self to awareness of the soul, and thus to start constructing the first span of the rainbow bridge or antahkarana. Arousing the Ajna chakra, the centre between the eyebrows, fosters the development of the intuition.

In Book II of the *Bhagavad Gita*, Krishna says:

> He who is united in soul-vision offers up even here both things well done and ill done; therefore, gird thyself for union with the Soul, for this union brings success in works.[12]

As this is achieved, it is then possible – following the stilling of the discursive mind, 'the chatter of the lower mentality' – to enter the silence and listen to the occasional whisper of the still small voice. In practice – certainly for the writer of this book – the process is anything but easy, and years and years of diligent effort may pass without obvious result. Yet something does happen. Slowly there is a change in attitude of mind, and intuitive insights – occasionally in flashes, more usually by slow and imperceptible degrees – do tend to occur rather more frequently.

In Book VI of the *Bhagavad Gita*, there is the following exchange between Arjuna and Krishna:

> Arjuna: 'This union through Oneness which is taught by Thee – I perceive not its firm foundation, owing to the wavering of the mind; for the mind wavers, Krishna, turbulent, impetuous, forceful; and I think it is hard to hold as the wind!'
>
> Krishna: 'Without doubt, mighty armed one, the wavering mind is hard to hold; but through assiduous practice, and through detachment it may be held firm. For him whose mind is uncontrolled, union is hard to obtain, this is my opinion; but for him whose mind has been brought under his sway, who is controlled, it can be won by the right means.'[13]

For readers unfamiliar with the practice of meditation two excellent books on the subject are *The Silent Path* by Michal J. Eastcott,[14] and *The Journey Inwards* by F. C. Happold.[15]

(e) 'Wanted for the building of the (New) Jerusalem, fewer architects more bricklayers.'

Almost everyone would agree that this country and the world generally face great problems. And the attitude of most people is that they would like to do what they can to help. So far so good. But then, all too often, come one or other of two comments. (i) 'I would like to do something. But what? In my position I feel so helpless.' Or (ii) 'If only . . .' – some variant of the theme that the grass on the other side of the fence is greener.

As an answer to (i) the Teacher in *The Wheel of Rebirth* points out:

> Speak peace, think peace, work unceasingly for peace. If your scope at first seems limited, do not despair, begin by

170

exerting your influence in your own immediate circle, and as your power for good grows, so will the circle widen about you. Exercise self-knowledge, self-judgment, and self-control; without these no progress can be made. Think right thoughts, refuse to be caught up in the vortex of fear and hate and greed which is raging about you. Seek to bring harmony into every life that touches yours; never stir up the embers of suspicion and of jealousy. Keep a guard over your tongue and let your thoughts be always positive, helpful and filled with love. Let each one refuse to listen to scandal or to repeat it whether it touches personal or national life. Remember ever, how mighty is the power of the Word.[16]

As a comment on (ii), Krishna says in the *Bhagavad Gita*:

Better one's own duty without excellence than the duty of another well followed out. Death in one's own duty is better; the duty of another is full of danger.[17]

(f) 'How many, impelled by motives seeming quite good to them, have sought, and sometimes even gained and used power to further some idea of progress, some forced modification of the people or circumstances around them. Did they know even a little of the working out in time of the causes they seek to launch, they would shrink from the responsibility involved.'

By implication this observation queries the wisdom of those who wish to bring about 'the forced modification'. Have they the necessary insight to know what is best for those on whom the modification is being imposed? About this Jung remarks:

Our social goals commit the error of overlooking the psychology of the person for whom they are intended and – very often – of promoting only his illusions.[18]

And in Chapter 2, p. 23, it was pointed out that changing conditions without a corresponding change in attitude of mind merely replaces one set of evils by another. But there is more to the above observation than that. Teachers are unanimous in emphasising the importance of respecting another's free-will. To suggest is entirely legitimate; to compel is not. To deny this freedom to normal adult human beings – an inevitable concomitant of totalitarian regimes – appears to break some spiritual law. And it is probably the implications of this law which underlie the statement: 'Did they know even a little of the working out in time of the causes they seek to launch, they would shrink from the responsibility involved.'

(g) 'It is infinitely more important to love our neighbour as ourselves (in the fullest meaning of the phrase) than to have the power to influence him without his knowledge and consent.'

The English language is said to be one of peculiar richness of word and phrase. This being so it is very strange that states and conditions which in other, and sometimes quite primitive, languages are defined by separate words, are all described in English by the one word love. Inevitably this has led on occasion to great confusion and much misunderstanding. So it is worth spending a little time examining the quite distinct states and conditions which are covered by the one word love. At the very least there are four. (i) Physical union: normally between members of the opposite sex; abnormally between members of the same sex. (ii) The glamorous and delightful (while it lasts) non-rational condition of being 'in love'. (iii) A feeling-thinking state of caring which is largely dependent on the reactions of the person cared for. (iv) A feeling-thinking state of caring which is largely independent of the reactions of the person cared for.[19] These states are not, of course, mutually exclusive.

At this point it is pertinent to enquire about the meaning to be given to the word love in the commandment 'Thou shalt love thy neighbour as thyself.' Remembering the context in which Jesus referred to this commandment – a lawyer's question and the parable of the Good Samaritan in reply – it is clear that loving our neighbour means having a deep and selfless concern – a concern moreover which embraces both thinking and feeling – for our neighbour's material, psychological and spiritual well-being. And our neighbour is 'everyman'. Love defined in this way is the state or condition referred to above as (iv). In this definition the crucial word is selfless; thus depicting a concern or caring which is largely independent of the reactions of the person cared for. A sublime example is the reaction of Jesus when being crucified. 'Father forgive them for they know not what they do.'[20] Even under those appalling conditions, Jesus' concern was for the spiritual well-being of his persecutors.

This vitally important subject of love will be considered further and from a different standpoint in the next chapter. An appropriate ending for this one is an Arab description of friendship:

> A true friend is one to whom you can tip out all the contents of your heart, chaff and grain together, knowing that the gentlest hands will take and sift it, keep what is worth keeping, and with the breath of kindness, blow the rest away.

References

1. *The Occult Way*, P. G. Bowen, (The Occult Book Society, 1938), Chap. III, p. 59
2. *The Undiscovered Self*, C. G. Jung, translated by R. F. C. Hull, (Routledge & Kegan Paul, 1958), Chap. IV, p. 56
3. *Education in the New Age*, Alice A. Bailey, (Lucis Press, 1954), p. 89
4. Luke 13:20, 21
5. *The New Man*, Maurice Nicoll, (Vincent Stuart, 1950), Chap. 1
6. John 3:1
7. *Bhagavad Gita*, translated with an introduction and commentary by Charles Johnston, (John M. Watkins, 1965), p. 57
8. *The Sayings of the Ancient One*, P. G. Bowen, (Rider & Co., 1935), Chap. V, Part I
9. *The Labours of Hercules*, Alice A. Bailey, (Lucis Press, 1974), Labour III, Part 1

10. *Ibid*. See Labour III, Part 2
11. *The Spiritual Path*, Raynor C. Johnson, (Hodder & Stoughton, 1972), p. 94
12. Same as ref. 7, Book II, v. 50
13. *Ibid*. Book VI, v. 33
14. *The Silent Path*, Michal J. Eastcott, (Rider & Co., 1969)
15. *The Journey Inwards*, F. C. Happold, (Darton, Longman & Todd, 1968)
16. *The Wheel of Rebirth*, H. K. Challoner, (Theosophical Publishing House, 1969. First published by Rider & Co., 1935), p. 282
17. Same as ref. 7, Book III, v. 35
18. Same as ref. 2, Chap. VII, p. 112
19. See *The Greater Awareness*, Cyril Scott, (George Routledge & Sons, 1936), Part 1
20. Luke 23:34

12: Virtue and Vice:
What it means to be good

Let every man sweep the snow from his own door, and not busy himself about the frost on his neighbour's tiles.

Chinese Proverb

He that knows not, and knows not that he knows not, is a fool – shun him.

He that knows not, and knows that he knows not, is a child – teach him.

He that knows, and knows not that he knows, is asleep – wake him.

He that knows, and knows that he knows, is wise – follow him.

Sufi Saying

The vices of men become steps on the ladder, one by one as they are surmounted. The virtues of men are steps indeed necessary, not by any means to be dispensed with, but though they create a fair atmosphere and a happy future they are useless if they stand alone.[1]

Light on the Path

Enter thy brother's heart and see his woe. Then speak. Let the words spoken convey to him the potent force he needs to loose his chains. Yet loose them not thyself. Thine is the work to speak with understanding. The force received by him will aid him in his work.

Enter thy brother's mind and read his thoughts, but only when thy thoughts are pure. Then think. Let the thoughts thus created enter thy brother's mind and blend with his. Yet keep detached thyself, for none have the right to sway a brother's mind. The only right there is will make him say: 'He loves. He standeth by. He knows. He thinks with me and I am strong to do the right.' Learn thus to speak. Learn thus to think.[2]

Two Rules

175

The title of this chapter was prompted by a remark sometimes heard among conventionally religious people: 'So and so is such a *good* person.' After hearing this observation rather *ad nauseam* many years ago, I began to wonder just what it was that a person so described was actually good for. After due reflection I came to the conclusion that about the only thing it did mean was that the individual in question did not appear to succumb to the more obvious weaknesses of the flesh. But whether from pure motives, i.e. motives that were selfless, or from impure motives, i.e. motives of vanity or fear – the desire to give a good impression, or fear of what people would say – was not clear. The more I thought about the matter, the less did it appear that mere abstention was sufficient to make someone good, and I was reminded of a saying and a story.

The saying: 'He is as good as gold and fit for Heaven, but of no earthly use.'

The story – of an Eastern Teacher: 'A weakly young man came to him, and said, "Master, I hear you have great wisdom, and I wish to study at your feet." The Teacher surveyed the young man. "Have you ever told a lie?" he asked. The young man, taken aback, replied, "No, Master, I have never told a lie." Back came the startling reply. "When you have learnt to tell a lie come and see me again." And the young man departed – perplexed and discomforted.'

The above is not to be taken as advocating sensuality and lying as desirable activities; that is *not* the moral to be drawn. What *is* being advocated is that the phrase 'being good' warrants more than conventional scrutiny.

At this point it is as well to distinguish between spiritual truths and moral laws. When the Yogi maintains 'All is Brahman', or the Hermeticist says 'God is all that was, all that is, and all that is to be', he believes he is stating a spiritual truth, such truths being permanent and unchanging. Moral laws on the other hand, and with them our ordinary conceptions of virtue and vice, are neither permanent nor unchanging. They depend upon circumstances, of which the two of greatest importance are the environing conditions, and the spiritual maturity of him who appraises and of him whose conduct is being appraised. For the same action may be virtuous when performed by one person on one occasion, but vicious when performed by a different person on a different occasion. Consider, for example, the moral codes which have governed the relations between men and women in different countries and at different periods of the world's history. The differences between them are immense.

What then is goodness? Are we to find that when subjected to analysis goodness disappears in a cloud of relativities and that the demons in the *Dream of Gerontius*[3] are right after all?

> Virtue and vice,
>   A knave's pretence,
>   'Tis all the same;
>   Ha! Ha!
>   Dread of hell-fire,
>   Of the venomous flame,
>   A coward's plea.
> Give him his price,
>   Saint though he be,
>   Ha! Ha!
> From shrewd good sense
>   He'll slave for hire;
>   Ha! Ha!
>   And does but aspire
> To the heaven above
>   With sordid aim
>   Not from love
>   Ha! Ha!

No! But what it does mean is that goodness can only be defined in relation to a given individual in a given place and at a given time, and that motive is all important.

After drafting this chapter, it was found that the four sections into which it naturally falls, correspond very closely with the qualifications for treading the path given in *At the*

Feet of the Master by Alcyone (Krishnamurti) – discrimination, desirelessness, good conduct, and love. So the sections have been headed accordingly.

Discrimination

To every man there openeth
A way, and ways, and a way.
And the High Soul climbs the High Way
And the Low Soul gropes the Low;
And in between, on the misty flats,
The rest drift to and fro.
But to every man there openeth
A High Way and a Low,
And every man decideth
The Way his Soul shall go.

John Oxenham

Picture a broad valley, flat and boggy, along which meanders a very winding river. The sides of the valley are rocky and precipitous, and the floor of the valley is covered with mist. Above the mist there is cloud, and above the cloud is sunshine. The object is to get into the sunshine, and there are three 'ways' of doing so. The first 'way' is up the path by the river. As this follows all the turns and twists of the river, progress is very slow. No particular qualities are called for by those who go this way. Indeed, the possession of special qualities is something of a disadvantage in that a marked characteristic of the people on this path is to say and do what those around them say and do. The three fundamental questions, 'Whence, why, and whither' evoke little interest, and are rarely discussed except superficially.

The second 'way' is, in fact, a multitude of ways. It includes all those who, because of boredom, curiosity, a longing for adventure, or some other reason, have become dissatisfied with the path by the river, and have made off over the mist-covered flats to the precipitous sides of the valley. But bogs and pools abound, and the going is tough.

The third 'way' refers to those who have crossed the flats and are climbing up the rocky sides of the valley. Some of the climbers are immersed in cloud; a few have pressed on through the cloud and are in sunshine.

The three 'ways' correspond closely to the three stages in the allegory of learning to drive a car (Chapter 7, p. 102). People on the path by the river (cf. Stage 1) give little thought to whether human life has meaning or purpose, their time and energy being devoted to their personal desires and wants. People crossing the misty flats (cf. Stage 2) feel that human life is indeed purposive, and their dominant concern is for the well-being of the whole. They are seekers; but to what end they do not know. People climbing the precipitous sides of the valley are those who have had a glimpse of the plan for humanity, and with imagination, devotion and insight, are striving to implement it (cf. Stage 3). In the sunshine are the Illuminati.

In this allegory, the state of development of an individual's consciousness is portrayed by the amount of climbing he has done, by his height above sea level. Sea level, appropriately enough, symbolises the emergence of individuality, the birth of man into the human kingdom. The journey up the valley and into the sunshine above the cloud represents man's journey through this kingdom.

Desirelessness

Crossing the flats corresponds to the growth, development and integration of the personality. Climbing the rocky and precipitous sides of the valley symbolises the conception, birth, and growth of the spiritual nature, and is achieved by transmuting personal desire into spiritual will, self-centred love into unconditional love and wisdom, and discursive thinking into intuitive insight and illumined understanding. Since transmutation is only possible when there is something to transmute, it follows that a personality which is both well developed and well integrated[4] is an essential prerequisite to

179

climbing the rocky and precipitous sides of the valley. About the spiritual nature P. G. Bowen writes as follows:

> To change his attitude towards, and outlook upon, life is the task which confronts the learner in True Occultism. He becomes a learner in all ways as unconscious of his spiritual selfhood as a newborn babe is of his human selfhood. The work, or duties of life; the conditions of life; and the contrasting facts of life and death oppose him with a challenge which he dimly feels he must accept if he is to become their master, and not remain their slave. They and their kindred bind and oppress him unceasingly; to realise this is the very first step. Weakness and ignorance are inseparable from the self-isolated nature, and with recognition of this comes understanding of the true nature of the effort required of him, namely to depose the personal selfhood and replace it by another. What the nature of this other consciousness may be he does not know, and for the time being may give it the negative name of impersonal.
>
> The great, ever-present problem confronting all who set themselves to travel this path is the conquest of desire. The more it is considered, the more difficult does it appear to one who thinks, but still lacks clear understanding. Desire, he perceives, is the great motive power of life, and if it be destroyed what can take its place? Without desire he thinks, and thinks rightly, there would be apathy and stagnation, but he fails to understand that DESIRE as a principle in universal nature is utterly different from human desires. The Desire Principle can no more be eliminated than can the universe, but human desires are simply the self-isolated consciousness functioning within this principle.
>
> As the learner eliminates (personal) desires by absorbing them into the one Desire to be Desireless, he finds himself more and more free to explore fresh fields of knowledge. Departments of the mind hitherto clouded and inactive spring into activity. A sense of peace comes as the ranks of warring desires become thinned. Poise becomes more and more assured as desire to stand apart from or above others fades away, and with it comes increasing knowledge of what true power means. Life grows fuller and richer as personal wants disappear. To this end, and to much more, the universal desire element

180

concentrated into a single stream and, no longer dissipating its force in a thousand meandering rivulets, bears the learner. It can, if no obstacle checks its flow, sweep him irresistibly through the blackness and silence which lie athwart the Threshold into the light of the spirit beyond.[5]

It is interesting to note the emphasis placed on this theme in a number of the world's great religions.

(a) Krishna – Thy right is to the work, but never to its fruits; let not the fruit of thy work be thy motive, nor take refuge in abstinence from works.[6]

(b) Hermetic Teaching – Labour always like one who seeks a Royal Reward for a task well done; but find your reward in work continued and never in work completed.[7]

(c) Gautama – And this, brethren, is the Ariyan Truth about the Ceasing of Suffering: Verily it is the utter passionless cessation of, the giving up, the forsaking, the release from, the absence of longing for, this Craving.[8]

(d) Seek ye the Kingdom of God; and all these things shall be added unto you.[9]

Good Conduct

As action springs from feeling and thinking, it follows that the source of right or wrong action, i.e. conduct, must be sought in right or wrong feeling and thinking. But before we can decide whether our feeling and thinking is right or wrong, we must be clear about the way in which we feel and think. We cannot afford to look at life through coloured spectacles or in the wrong direction. An essential prerequisite is therefore emotional detachment and intellectual honesty. If we observe ourselves with the clarity of vision which these two qualities provide, we may become aware that the garden of our minds contains two rampageous weeds: liana, a creeper which chokes everything within its reach – vanity; and bindweed, another creeper but one which travels underground and so is harder to eradicate – spiritual pride. If we have the moral courage to be honest with ourselves, we may be surprised by

181

the extent to which our actions or, what is more fundamental, the feelings and thoughts which give rise to them, depend on our attempt to be thought well of either by others or by ourselves, instead of on the basic principles which alone can determine whether an action is good or bad. The wording on a wayside pulpit is very apt in this connection: 'Concentrate on being better than you look instead of on looking better than you are.' And much of that inspired Eastern Scripture, the *Bhagavad Gita*, is concerned with just this point.

What follows is adapted from Chapter III of *The Occult Way* by P. G. Bowen.[10]

To live virtuously is to live in harmony with life, i.e. according to the laws of universal nature. To do this involves the practice of the following ten virtues. They fall into two sets of five, of which the second set (vi)–(x) is the complement of the first set (i)–(v).

(i)	Harmlessness	(−)	(vi)	Charity	(+)
(ii)	Truthfulness	(+)	(vii)	Contentment	(−)
(iii)	Justice	(−)	(viii)	Discrimination	(+)
(iv)	Purity	(+)	(ix)	Simplicity	(−)
(v)	Self-reliance	(+)	(x)	Self-surrender	(−)

Though each of these virtues is predominantly positive or predominantly negative, each has both a positive and negative aspect. A virtue is exhibited most completely when there is a balance between its positive and negative manifestations. There follows a brief commentary on the first four of these ten virtues.

Harmlessness

Harmlessness is a negative virtue, of which Charity is the positive counterpart. Like all virtues it manifests in two aspects, positive and negative. In its negative aspect it manifests as restraint from doing harm; in its positive aspect as the prevention of harm from being done. So that man is most harmless when he refrains equally from inflicting harm and from permitting harm to be inflicted. One example which merits reflection is the problem presented by pacifism. Most pacifists concentrate on the negative aspect of harmlessness and take little or no note of its positive aspect. If they did so their decision might be different.

Truthfulness

Truthfulness is a positive virtue of which Contentment is the negative counterpart. 'To express reality is to be truthful; to accept it is to be content.' As with Harmlessness man is most truthful when he equally tells the truth and causes the truth to be told. If this is thought to be a platitude, it is worth pondering the well known aphorism: 'Speak truth when compelled to speak; it not, keep silence.'

What follows is an extract from a statement made recently by the Teacher referred to in Chapters 7 and 8.

Today the greatest drawback to progress in your world is the spoken word of half-truth. This has become a danger that is not noticed because it is becoming so prevalent. Half-truths spoken by men who are in places of power and influence, half-truths printed in your newspapers, your books; half-truths spoken by men who have no intention of speaking the truth, but who are cloaking their words that they may be taken in two ways. These half-truths are spoken by men who should be men of integrity. And they are half-lies because the very men and women who utter them have no intention of fulfilling what they say. They come from shallow minds, from self-seeking minds, from power-struck minds who have lost the compassion, love, loyalty and beauty, that have made this civilisation.

When you have found what is authentic truth to your mind and soul, speak it and then live it. There is in the world today this speaking one way and living another. My friends, this brings disaster. The new age will not be realised until men learn to speak what is true.

In your country there is not today that same anger against truth. There will not be death for truth speakers as there used to be, but there is the more subtle way of ridicule and of criticism.

That is a certain way of stopping the truth being spoken. In other countries there is of course the way of imprisonment for those who speak the truth. All these half-truths are building up into what may become a great and dreadful holocaust. My friends, learn to live the truth, for there will be no other way of living and thinking when you leave the physical body. You will not then be able to think in half-truths, for truth will show, will be made manifest. Therefore have the strength, the realisation to say now that which is true.

Justice

Of the real meaning of justice it seems that we can only have a limited conception at our present stage of evolution. For consider the following hypothetical problem. A man is given a sum of money by a friend (who stipulates anonymity) and is asked to apportion it as justly as he can between three individuals whom we will call A, B and C. After agreeing to do this, he discovers to his dismay that A is a rascal and in need, that B is relatively honest but completely ineffective, and that C is eminently worthy and with a more than adequate income. After considering the problem with which his friend has confronted him, he realises that he has no principles on which to decide what to do. If he takes purely material standards of need as his guide, he will decide to give most to A, some to B, and little or none to C. If he takes moral worth as his guide, he will distribute the money in exactly the reverse manner. But if he works on the assumption that according to the Good Law – karma – these three men have already had perfect justice meted out to them, he will divide the sum into three equal amounts. What justice is he does not know.

Purity

When considering the virtues, it must always be borne in mind that experience is the food of real being, and that without experience growth is impossible. Knowledge (not to be confused with mere information) is food which has been digested, experience that has been assimilated. Experience that the being is capable of assimilating into knowledge, or that stimulates being into healthy activity, is pure; all other forms are impure in one degree or another. Idle habits, restless pursuits of fresh interests and sensations, are impure forms of experience; the first because they are but empty husks, the second because they are usually unassimilable, and in bulk far in excess of requirements.

A sincere and fearless application of the preceding virtues to the problems of everyday life is usually instructive and often helpful. It will not normally provide a neat solution to the problem, nor will it normally remove the suffering which the problem may be causing – on occasions it may even enhance it – but it does provide a firm foothold from which to take the next step. Applying the virtues corresponds to the use of a compass by a traveller lost in a forest. The way to the edge of the forest may mean leaving a partial clearing and diving into the undergrowth, but the traveller does at least know that if he can keep going in the direction indicated by the compass bearing he will eventually reach the edge of the forest and enter open country. If all else fails, help is sometimes forthcoming by meditating on the mystic phrase 'The Path of Natural Duty'.

Love

Thou shalt love thy neighbour as thyself

I once asked the Bishop of Geneva what one must do to attain perfection. 'You must love God with all your heart,' he answered, 'and your neighbour as yourself.' 'I did not ask wherein perfection lies,' I rejoined, 'but how to attain it.' 'Charity,' he said again, 'that is both the means and the end, the only way by which we can reach that perfection which is, after all, but Charity itself.' 'I know all that,' I said. 'But I want to know how one is to love God with all one's heart and one's

185

neighbour as oneself.' But again he answered, 'We must love God with all our hearts, and our neighbour as ourselves.' 'I am no further than I was,' I replied. 'Tell me how to acquire such love.' 'The best way, the shortest and easiest way of loving God with all one's heart is to love Him wholly and heartily!' He would give no other answer. At last, however, the Bishop said, 'There are many besides you who want me to tell them of methods and systems and secret ways of becoming perfect, and I can only tell them that the sole secret is a hearty love of God, and the only way of attaining that love is by loving. You learn to speak by speaking, to study by studying, to run by running, to work by working; and just so you learn to love God and man by loving.[11]

Of the four qualities referred to in this chapter – discrimination, desirelessness, good conduct and love – love is the most important. For by cultivating love, the other qualities may be acquired; but the converse is not true. At the end of Chapter 11 it was pointed out that the word love has several distinct meanings, and that failure to distinguish between them has led to great confusion. Perhaps the most vital difference is between love which is conditional, that is, love which is largely governed by the reaction of the person(s) loved; and love which is unconditional, that is love which is largely independent of the reaction of the person(s) loved. Such love is certainly coloured by feeling, but it wells up from our innermost being and is independent of circumstances and reciprocity. It is rooted in the love of God 'the Father of Lights with whom can be no variation, neither shadow that is cast by turning',[12] and it is this kind of love which is referred to in the second commandment. But before we can run, we must have learnt how to walk! Hence the tremendous importance of cultivating love – a deep sense of caring – as part of our ordinary consciousness. To start with we can learn to love the people whom we naturally take to and who probably reciprocate our love. We can make the love that we feel part of our very being so that we unconsciously radiate it to all around us. Then, and much harder, we can learn to love those people whom we do not naturally take to and who may not reciprocate our love. At this stage a real danger is to part company with wisdom and common sense and incur the plea of Mrs Smith to her vicar about frequent and not too welcome visits from Mrs Jones: 'Vicar, will you please stop Mrs Jones saving her soul through me.' Eventually, wise, sincere and sustained efforts along these lines may result in a momentary flooding of the consciousness by spiritual love, a sense of mystical union with all that lives. As part of normal consciousness such a condition lies for most of us in the far distant future, but flashes we can and do have now. It is the universal nature of such love that prompted the use of the word 'impersonal' in the quotation on p. 180.

Paul's description of love in his letter to the Corinthians has probably never been surpassed and, in spite of being so well known, provides a fitting end to this chapter.

> If I speak with the tongues of men and of angels, and have not love, I am become sounding brass, or a clanging cymbal. And if I have the gift of prophecy, and know all mysteries and all knowledge; and if I have all faith, so as to remove mountains, but have not love, I am nothing. And if I bestow all my goods to feed the poor, and if I give my body to be burned, but have not love, it profiteth me nothing. Love suffereth long, and is kind; love envieth not; love vaunteth not itself, is not puffed up, doth not behave itself unseemly, seeketh not its own, is not provoked, taketh not account of evil; rejoiceth not in unrighteousness, but rejoiceth with the truth; beareth all things, believeth all things, hopeth all things, endureth all things. Love never faileth.[13]

References

1. *Light on the Path*, written down by Mabel Collins, (Theosophical Publishing House, 1920). Commentary on rule 20 in Chap. 1
2. *A Treatise on White Magic*, Alice A. Bailey, (Lucis Publishing Co., 5th edition, 1951. First published 1934), p. 320

3. *Dream of Gerontius*, Cardinal Newman, Section IV
4. cf. The analogy on p. 165 of Chap. 11
5. *The Sayings of the Ancient One*, P. G. Bowen, (Rider, 1935), Chap. V, Part II
6. *Bhagavad Gita*, translated with an introduction and commentary by Charles Johnston, (John M. Watkins, 1965), Book II, v. 47 & 48
7. Ref. 5, Chap. III, p. 31
8. *Some Sayings of the Buddha*, translated by F. L. Woodward, (Oxford University Press, World's Classics Edition, 1951. First published 1925)
9. Luke 12:31
10. *The Occult Way*, P. G. Bowen, (The Occult Book Society, 1938), Chap. III
11. *The Perennial Philosophy*, Aldous Huxley, (Chatto & Windus, 1946), p. 104
12. James 1:17
13. 1 Corinthians 13:1

13: Evil, Sin and Suffering

All Truth is a shadow, except the last, except the utmost; yet every Truth is true in its kind. It is substance in its own place, though it be but a shadow in another place (for it is but a reflection from an intenser substance); and the shadow is a true shadow, as the substance is a true substance.[1]

Isaac Pennington

Our highest truths are but half-truths. Think not to settle down forever in any truth. Make use of it as a tent in which to pass a summer's night. But build no house of it, or it will be your tomb. When you first have an inkling of its insufficiency and begin to descry a dim counter-truth looming up beyond, then weep not, but give thanks. It is the Lord's voice whispering: 'Take up thy bed and walk.'[2]

A. J. Balfour

Realise that actually there is no such thing as punishment. It is a man-made term, for what is in truth a law of profoundest love, whereby humanity learns through experience to associate effects with their causes.[3]

A Teacher

It is better by far to err through ignorance than to do right blindly at the direction of another. For in the first instance, the person learns his error through experience of its effects and so profits. But in the second, the person learns nothing at all, and suffers in one degree or another through abandonment of individual responsibility.[4]

P. G. Bowen

189

Sin and Evil

For the writer to comment on sin and evil when so much has been written about these two topics by professional philosophers and theologians may seem presumptuous. Maybe it is! The writer's excuse for doing so is the vital importance of these two subjects and the fact that so much that has been written by the professionals is too erudite to be read and understood by the ordinary layman. There is confusion, too, because the words sin and evil are used in so many different senses. That there are at least three distinct categories of sin and evil is shown by the following very simple example.

Smith, Jones and Robinson, are three people. Jones is responsible to Smith; Robinson knows both Smith and Jones but is responsible to neither.

Case (i)   Robinson tells Smith that he is treating Jones badly. Smith had not realised the fact, agrees, is sorry, and decides to treat Jones differently in future.
An example of *unconscious sin*,[5] followed by repentance.

Case (ii)   Smith loses his temper and treats Jones badly. Smith is fully aware of what he has done, is sorry, and determines to behave better in future.
An example of *conscious sin*, followed by repentance.

Case (iii)   Smith treats Jones badly, knowingly and deliberately, because he wishes to reduce Jones to a condition of impotent servitude.
An example of *evil*.

In the New Testament the Greek word translated sin – *hamartano* – means 'missing the mark' (literally, in archery when the target is missed); and the Greek word translated repentance – *metanoia* – means 'change of mind'.[6] Cases (i) and (ii) are examples of missing the mark. But the existence of the mark, the target, is not in question. A penetrating example of these two kinds of sin is Jesus' account of the publican and the Pharisee praying in the Temple.[7] The

190

publican knew perfectly well that he was a sinner and wanted to be better (otherwise he would not have been in the Temple). With him it was a case of 'For the good that I would I do not; but the evil which I would not, that I practise.'[8]

The Pharisee was probably hard-working, honest in his relations with others but not with himself, and a stalwart upholder, both in theory and practice, of the then existing moral code. In fact, he was almost certainly a much 'better' man than the publican in every respect save one. He was spiritually proud. He lacked the humility without which all other virtues turn sour. He thought he had 'arrived', and that there was little left for him to learn.

> What modern hearers may miss is how shocking the story must have sounded in the ears of its first hearers. The Pharisee stood out among his fellow-men, just as he stood apart in the temple court, for his high moral character. His life was a continual protest against low standards, whether in commercial or domestic life. Dishonesty in finance or disloyalty in the home were abhorrent to him. Nor was he content – as many are today – with a sound ethic divorced from religion. Where the law required one annual fast, he fasted twice weekly. He gave tithes of all that he bought. He did not ascribe all this to his own efforts, but was ready to give thanks to God for his achievements.
>
> The picture of the tax-gatherer at prayer, sketched by Jesus in a few deft strokes, is indelibly printed on Christian minds. He stands on the extreme edge of the worshipping crowd, his eyes downcast, his hands not lifted in adoration, but engaged in 'beating his breast' the seat of sin, as he thought. But it is this prayer which, according to Jesus, wins God's verdict of free forgiveness. The Pharisee was grateful to God, but his very gratitude showed how far he was from a true understanding of God's nature. Instead of sensing God's infinite holiness, he came into His presence with his mind concentrated on his own virtues.
>
> An extract from *The Times* of many years ago.

In Case (iii), the target of Cases (i) and (ii) is rejected, and a very different target – the ruthless pursuit of selfish power, completely unrelieved by love – is put in its place. Those

who have made this decision, in full awareness of what they
are doing, have chosen the left hand path. Such people have
set their face against 'returning to the centre' (see Chapter 9,
p. 138), and are determined 'to rule in hell rather than serve
in heaven'.[9]

Now comes the fearful problem. If God (however thought
of) is good, whence comes evil? The problem is put very
clearly by J. J. van der Leeuw in *The Conquest of Illusion*.

> How can a Creator be omnipotent and good and yet create
> evil or allow it to originate? Either God created evil with the
> intention to do so, in which case we cannot call Him good, or
> else He could not help creating it or, even worse, evil has an
> objective existence apart from the divine Being, eternally
> opposed to him, in both of which cases we can hardly call God
> omnipotent. It does not help us to say, as is often done, that he
> gave free will to man, power to choose either good or evil, and
> that man chose wrongly. If man could choose wrongly that
> inclination for evil must have been created in him; had he been
> created all good, he could only have chosen good, and thus the
> problem remains the same. Even less can we look upon man's
> deliberate choice of evil as an unforeseen misfortune in the
> scheme of things, something of which the Creator had not
> thought; in that case where is divine omniscience?[10]

The appalling difficulty is the seemingly utter incompati-
bility of evil with a God who is both all-loving and all-
powerful. But what do we mean by all-powerful? Does it
mean that we credit God with the capacity to do literally
anything, including for example making two plus two equal
five? Scarcely. Then may it not be the case that there is only
one path to God's goal for mankind, and that that path is
along the valley in the shadow of evil and suffering? If God's
goal for man is a being who is proof against committing evil
by intent or by mistake while at the same time having
complete freewill, it is at least arguable that immunity
against committing evil can only be obtained by committing
evil and experiencing its results. Perhaps the supreme
qualities of love, loyalty and courage, can only be acquired

in a world in which there is evil, pain and suffering. Such thinking underlies the following remarkable poem, *The Fullness of Time*, by the Irish mystic poet James Stephens (1882–1950).

> On a rusty iron throne,
> Past the furthest star of space,
> I saw Satan sit alone,
> Old and haggard was his face;
> For his work was done; and he
> Rested in eternity.
>
> And to him from out the sun
> Came his father and his friend
> Saying, – Now the work is done
> Enmity is at an end –
> And he guided Satan to
> Paradises that He knew.
>
> Gabriel, without a frown;
> Uriel, without a spear;
> Raphael came singing down,
> Welcoming their ancient peer;
> And they seated him beside
> One who had been crucified!

Maybe devising a path without the possibility of evil and suffering would involve a fundamental inconsistency or contradiction, and so is an impossibility, even for God? Perhaps the following quotation from a trance writing given through Dr Anna Kingsford says all that can be said, be it much or little, at our present stage of development.

> You have demanded also the origin of evil . . . Understand then that Evil is the result of Creation. For Creation is the result of the projection of Spirit into matter; and with this projection came the first germ of evil. We would have you know that there is no such thing as a purely spiritual evil, but evil is the result of the materialisation of Spirit. If you examine carefully all we have said to you concerning the various forms of evil, you will see that every one is the result of the limitation of the power to

193

perceive that the whole Universe is but the Larger Self . . . It is, then, true that God created evil; but yet it is true that God is Spirit, and being Spirit is incapable of evil. Evil is then purely and solely the result of the materialisation of God. This is a great mystery . . . God is universal percipience. God is that which sees and that which is seen. If we could see all, hear all, touch all, and so forth, there would be no evil, for evil comes of the limitation of perception. Such limitation was necessary if God was to produce aught other than God. Aught other than God must be less than God. Without evil, therefore, God would have remained alone. All things are God according to the measure of the Spirit in them.[11]

For Discussion

1.   I am the Lord, and there is none else. I form the light, and create darkness; I make peace, and create evil; I am the Lord, that doeth all these things.

Isaiah 45:6, 7

2.   The law of polarity was for Heraclitus, the Logos, the inner thought, or supreme principle of the Cosmos. All energies had their contraries, and from the strain their opposition engendered the world had arisen. In a word, no opposition, no world. These rival forces were, in fact, the two inseparable halves of the same thing, as are the concave and convex sides of a curve, they were contrary yet complementary activities, which by their union in disunion produce an attunement, a hidden harmony, better than an open and evident. For that which strives against another in reality supports itself. As heat implies cold, justice implies injustice. Sickness it is which makes health desirable, fatigue gives sweetness to rest, evil is the buttress of good. We may go further and say things produce their opposites, good sets up a counter-current of evil and evils give rise to good.[12]

The Human Situation by W. Macneile Dixon

3.   The problem of the opposites is for Jung 'a law inherent in human nature'. 'The psyche is a self-regulating system.' And 'There is no equilibrium and no self-regulating system without opposition.'[13]

The Psychology of C. G. Jung by Dr Jolan Jacobi

194

Suffering

What follows is in no sense an 'answer' to the problem of suffering. All that is claimed for the views expressed is that they indicate an approach which may prove helpful. We shall begin by considering human suffering, and shall end with some observations about the suffering of animals.

The dictionary defines suffering as the bearing of pain. To the question 'What causes pain?' the answer is '*Dis*harmony'. But disharmony and the pain to which it gives rise can exist on many different levels – physical, emotional, intellectual and spiritual. And there can be, and often is, disharmony on several levels at the same time. Indeed, emotional and intellectual disharmony usually occur together. Two observations are now pertinent.

First, the causes of pain and disharmony fall into two categories. (a) The sudden and unexpected – for example, an accident, or somebody's death. (b) The long drawn-out and foreseen – for example, prolonged illness, or the gradual sapping of hope regarding some aim or objective. In connection with (a), fear – fear of what will happen – plays little or no part. Because 'it', whatever 'it' may be, has already happened. But for events in category (b) it is different. What the future will bring forth may, and often does, play a crucial role in enhancing suffering.[14]

Second, experiences causing pain and disharmony are of two kinds. (α) Those which can manifestly lead to growth towards spiritual maturity, for example, illness resulting from an unwise mode of living, or the collapse of some self-centred ambition. (β) Those which, on the face of it, are unlikely so to lead, for example acute physical pain during a protracted terminal illness, or the loss through accident of a much loved only child to parents who had had to wait many years for one. The use of the phrase 'on the face of it' is deliberate, because there are people who have undergone such experiences and who, by the exercise of immense courage, have become a cause for wonder and a source of

195

inspiration.[15] But such people are exceptional. For many, such experiences are destructive. Among experiences which, on the face of it, would be unlikely to lead to growth, are the hideous blots on human history represented by the tens of thousands of men and women who were thrown to the lions in the Colosseum in Rome nearly 2000 years ago, and the hundreds of thousands of men, women and children who were tortured and then murdered in Nazi concentration camps before and during World War II. These events involved suffering as intense as any known to man because the suffering was on all levels and was deliberately fanned by fear. Of the victims, some of the Christians (and others) in the Colosseum and some of the Jews (and others) in the concentration camps displayed qualities of such outstanding greatness that one can but bow one's head in homage. But for many, predictably, it was different. What happened in a particular situation is illustrated very clearly by that splendid and most moving book, subsequently produced as a play *The Diary of Anne Frank.*

Now what are we to say when confronted by this vast and ever-present picture of suffering, both of the individual and of the group? How is this to be squared – can it indeed be squared – with proposition 6 at the end of Chapter 6, 'Love, justice, and perfection exist at the heart of the universe'?

The answer to the question is 'Yes, it can', but only when suffering is considered in conjunction with the long-term purpose of the school of human life, namely 'That it should educate its pupils to perform whatever parts they are called upon to play in the drama of life with grace, skill and selfless dedication.' For the learning process involves trial and error and making mistakes – going through school without ever making a mistake is inconceivable! – and sooner or later mistakes involve suffering. Moreover, I *suspect* that this applies throughout all manifestation and at levels which far transcend the human. For with manifestation is associated becoming, and becoming implies learning, and learning involves trial and error and making mistakes.

A question of some importance is 'How would a

spiritually mature human being – one who is approaching the end of the human journey – react under experiences which have been referred to as unlikely to lead to growth?' About the answer to that question there can be no doubt: he would shine as a light in the darkness, Jesus for example. We are thus left with the problem of those who, through no fault of their own, get caught up in some mass movement and end up in an environment such as a concentration camp which demands from them more than they have got in terms of qualities of character.

Let us consider an allegory; three scenes in the life of a human being. The first when a young child; the second, when an adolescent; the third, when a fully grown man or woman.

The first scene shows a child in a play-pen, learning to walk. After careful observation we note the following:

(i)   That progress, i.e. the ability to walk, consists in the capacity to overcome difficulties, for example not overbalancing when the side of the play-pen is out of reach or of tripping over Teddy who is lying on the floor, and that the required ability is only achieved by facing up to, and actually overcoming, these difficulties.

(ii)   That no progress can be made without risk, and therefore without the possibility of error and the attendant suffering.

(iii)   That the potentialities for both progress and error are restricted by the size of the play-pen.

(iv)   That for the child the actual process of learning to walk is largely unconscious; the logical connection between acting in one way and succeeding, or acting in another way and suffering, being only realised, and then not consciously, very slowly.

On endeavouring to see if there is any way by which the child can avoid suffering, we are forced to the conclusion that there is not – except for a brief period. Only during the time when the limitation (for example not being able to walk) associated with a particular cycle of learning has been transcended (for example by the ability to walk) and another cycle of learning has not yet begun is there a period of harmony, and hence an absence of suffering. But this condition, however delightful, cannot be preserved indefinitely, any more than can a perfectly ripe fruit, for change is fundamental to all that lives.

And what is the state of mind of the parents while this is going on? Two points seem worthy of mention:

(i)   The parents adjust – and this means increasing just as often as decreasing – the child's difficulties to what the child can reasonably be expected to overcome (for example by dangling before the child something that he wants and getting him to stand without holding on to the side of the play-pen).

(ii)   The parents are not normally very upset when the child makes a mistake (for example tripping over Teddy) and suffers (for example bumping his head against the side of the play-pen).

But accidents can and do happen. It may involve only the child, for example the child falls over and by some mischance does itself a serious injury; an unlikely event, but not unknown. Or it may involve the child as an unwitting member of the local community; for example a disturbance takes place, in the course of which a stone is thrown through a window of the child's bedroom, and a glass splinter enters one of the child's eyes; very unlikely, but not impossible. What happens? The parents are involved, fully and at once. They, and not only they, will do all they can, both at the time and subsequently, to offset the effects of the accident. May there not be some parallel here with the concentration camp experience? Is it not probable that every effort will be made by those whose responsibility it is – maybe after death and by the conditions of a subsequent incarnation – to offset the disintegrative effect of the concentration camp experience?

In the second and third scenes, i.e. those of adolescence and manhood or womanhood, the 'ring-pass-not' – the boundary of the play-pen in scene (i) – has been progressively pushed back, and the kind of difficulties to be overcome are, of course, very different, being emotional and mental rather than physical. Even so, the observations made in connection with scene (i) still largely apply. In fact, the only differences of real substance are that the process of learning has become progressively more conscious, and the effort to manifest the pattern of manhood or womanhood has become deliberate.

Regarding things of the spirit the analogy between the spiritually ignorant and the child in its play-pen is remarkably close. The child learns by trial and error and largely unconsciously. So for the most part do we. The child hits its head on the side of the play-pen and suffers, having failed to notice that Teddy was lying on the floor and would have to be stepped over. We, for our part, frequently wonder 'what has hit us' and why we should suffer, being almost completely unaware of the spiritual laws that we have broken by our uncontrolled and misdirected thoughts and emotions. For it has been suggested that with thoughts and emotions are associated subtle forces and energies, and just as in the case of forces and energies in the physical world, these can be transformed but not destroyed. With a feeling of hatred, for instance, is associated a subtle energy which will be destructive until transmuted by love. May this not be why Jesus said 'Love your enemies, do good to them that hate you, bless them that curse you, pray for them that despitefully use you'? Moreover if an ancient teaching is correct which states that the forces and energies associated with thoughts and feelings which are self-centred return eventually to the individual who sent them forth,[16] is it really surprising that we suffer as we do when so many of our thoughts and feelings are, or have been in the past, self-centred and destructive.[17]

Between the spiritual learner and the adolescent there is also a close analogy. Learning is now a conscious process, and the laws governing thought and emotion are one of the subjects studied. Spiritual perception begins to grow, and life's pattern, apparently so unjust and inexplicable, starts to be illumined by the eye of the spirit.

About the state of consciousness which characterises the spiritually wise it is pointless to speculate as it is as different from that with which we are familiar as the consciousness of the full grown man or woman differs from that of the child in its play-pen.

Now what can we say about 'Nature red in tooth and claw' – the suffering which animals inflict on each other. Most people find this topic embarrassing, but for that very reason it is important to be objective and not to endow animals with the thoughts and feelings appropriate to a human being. With the partial exception of domestic animals, such as cats, dogs and horses, it is very doubtful whether animals experience suffering other than of a purely physical kind. Among animals, fear is instinctive fear. 'Fear of what the future will bring forth' appears to be an essentially human quality. But physical suffering there is indeed. What are we to make of a 'bloated' sheep, capsized and unable to right itself, and crows taking advantage of its helplessness to eat, peck by peck, its eyes. It is not a question of cruelty, as what the crows do they do by instinct. But such occurrences, in which nature abounds, do leave in most people a feeling of unease. That there is no simple and satisfactory answer to the problem is all too clear. For humans it was found essential to consider suffering in the context of 'the long term purpose of the school of human life'. Could not something comparable hold good in the case of animals? But now comes the difficulty. What is the long-term purpose of animal life on this planet? To what end is it evolving? At present we simply do not know. But by analogy with human suffering, it may well be that for animals, physical suffering, though undesirable in itself, is an unavoidable concomitant of the long-term purpose for the animal kingdom. On such a matter, and with due regard to our present state of ignorance, it is wise to keep a very open mind.

EVIL, SIN AND SUFFERING

Explicitly in *A Treatise on Cosmic Fire*,[18] obliquely in *The Secret Doctrine*,[19] there are hints that in its early stages the evolutionary scheme for humanity was involved in a systemic failure, and that in consequence conditions on this planet are both more material, and suffering is greater, than originally envisaged. It is also asserted that within the Solar System the Earth is referred to as 'The Sorrowful Planet' or 'The Sphere of Suffering'. Strange though this seems, perhaps it is indeed the case!

For Discussion

The human being has a possibility consciously to take life in hand. You have all the lower kingdoms contained within you and you have the possibility to make all these kingdoms participators in this conscious life. Therefore you are indeed sons of God. It is, however, a struggle which is very difficult for you by reason of your having the three lower kingdoms within you, with all the aggressive drives which have been necessary for their survival and for the propagation of the species. But you are also spirit and life, and you have the possibility to transform instinct into intuition, sexual drive into the experience of oneness, and the sense of pleasure into joyfulness and bliss.

All you therefore experience in the form of struggle and suffering is in reality providing you with the possibility to transform into this new life, where there is none of the suffering which you experience now. But understand that everything you now experience is in a sense natural for that battlefield upon which you find yourself at this moment, and I would ask you not to despair because of the pain which you experience.

You are in a struggle between the lower and the higher expressions of life. You have entered this condition of your own free will and you are precisely where you have chosen to be. On the one hand there is attachment to the old forms, and on the other a resurrection into a new life in a new form. The only real error is in isolating yourself, and above all in hindering others from opening up to life. Don't judge. Work, work and be God in action.[20]

Gita Keiller

201

As long as you have your attention fixed more on life in a form than on Life Itself, you will always experience suffering. Ponder on this.[21]

Gita Keiller

References

1. *The Life of a Christian*, Isaac Pennington, 1653. First page (unnumbered)
2. Quoted by Eric Abbott, Dean of Westminster, at a service marking the end of the Abbey's 90th anniversary year (1966)
3. *The Wheel of Rebirth*, H. K. Challoner, (Theosophical Publishing House, 1969. First published by Rider, 1935), p. 55
4. *The Sayings of the Ancient One*, P. G. Bowen, (Rider & Co.), p. 72
5. See *Conscious and Unconscious Sin*, R. E. D. Clark, (Williams & Norgate, 1934)
6. *The Mark*, Maurice Nicoll, (Vincent Stuart, 1954), p. 87
7. Luke 18:9
8. Romans 7:19
9. *The Occult Way*, P. G. Bowen, (The Occult Book Society, 1938), p. 195
10. *The Conquest of Illusion*, J. J. van der Leeuw, (Allen & Unwin, 1928), p. 140
11. *A Treatise on Cosmic Fire*, Alice A. Bailey, (Lucis Press, 1925), p. 835
12. *The Human Situation*, W. Macneile Dixon, (Edward Arnold & Co., 1946. First published 1937), p. 199
13. *The Psychology of C. G. Jung*, Jolan Jacobi, (Kegan Paul, Trench, Trubner & Co., Third edition 1944. First published 1942), p. 50
14. *What of Tomorrow?*, H. K. Challoner, (Theosophical Publishing House, 1976)
15. See *Summons to Life*, Martin Israel, (Hodder & Stoughton, 1974), Chap. 8
16. See *The Secret Science Behind Miracles*, Max Freedom Long, (Huna Research Publications, Vista, California, 1948)
17. See *The Path of Healing*, H. K. Challoner, (Theosophical Publishing House, 1972. First published by Rider, 1938)

202

18. Same as ref. 11, p. 416
19. *The Secret Doctrine*, H. P. Blavatsky, Adyar Edition, (Theosophical Publishing House, 1950. First published 1888). Vol. I, p. 97 (Stanza 6, sloka 5); Vol. III, p. 106, 107 Vol. IV, p. 84
20. *Let Life Live*, Gita Keiller, (The Mitre Press, 1975), p. 10
21. *Ibid*. p. 6

14: The Fruit of Experience

You should not cry to God. The wellspring is in you. If you
do not block the outlet, the spring will flow and flow.[1]

Angelus Silesius

God grant me the serenity
To accept the things I cannot change;
The courage to change the things I can;
And the wisdom to know the difference.[2]

Christoph Oetinger (1702–82)

Perfectly to will what God wills, to want what he wants, is
to have joy; but if one's will is not quite in unison with God's,
there is no joy.[3]

Meister Eckhart

In the last chapter we considered evil, sin and suffering, and
saw that their existence is not, of itself, inconsistent with the
proposition that 'Love, Justice and Perfection exist at the
heart of the Universe'. In arriving at this conclusion we saw
that suffering and disharmony are intimately linked.

It is time now to consider joy and happiness, and why it is
that these two qualities are not more abundantly in
evidence. A little reflection indicates that for any particular
person at any given time the key factor is the presence or
absence of harmony. For in general terms the former implies
happiness, and the latter indicates its lack. Is the person all
of a piece and at peace with himself; or is he all pieces, and
full of conflicting thoughts and feelings? If the latter – why?
For what reason? Questions which the Buddha considered in
his first sermon.

Put in its simplest terms, the Buddha's answer to the

204

question 'Why? For what reason?' is 'Personal desire – I wish or I want, or I don't wish or I don't want – for myself.' And his advice? To follow the Eight-fold Path, the Noble Middle Way – right view, right aim, right speech, right action, right living, right effort, right mindfulness, right contemplation.[4] What does this mean today for the ordinary man or woman of well-to-do countries in the Western World?

In spite of the 2500 years which have elapsed since the Buddha taught and the very different conditions in which most people in the Western World now live their lives, the points made in that first sermon are as relevant today as they were then. To start with it is very important to realise the difference between needs and wants. If a person or family lacks adequate food, clothing, shelter and medical attention, they are in need and there is suffering – a condition which applies to at least half the world's present population. About this, and its undesirability, there can be no question. Nor can it be questioned that to tolerate the continued existence of people and families in such conditions constitutes a serious indictment of the community of which they are members. *But once basic needs are met, the situation changes.* A gap appears between needs and wants, and as material standards rise, the size of the gap increases. In the normal way the law of diminishing returns should start to operate. Maybe it does, but only to a limited extent. For the psychological pressures to which we are all subject, and which are aimed at enlarging and inflaming our wants, and at making us think that what we want we need, are enormous. Moreover, these pressures are such an integral part of the psychological climate in which we live that we rarely question their existence. What, you may ask, has all this got to do with happiness? The answer is 'A great deal'. Because behind these pressures is the implication that happiness depends on the possession of things, and can therefore be bought. Whereas a little reflection shows that once basic needs are met happiness depends on nothing of the kind, but

205

on our attitude to life – human, animal and what is embraced by the word nature. Startling as it may seem, and contrary to what is implicitly but generally maintained, the present attitude to material growth which permeates the affluent countries of the Western World is not well calculated to increase the sum total of human happiness in those countries. In *Let Life Live* a Teacher, communicating telepathically through Gita Keiller, says:

> The society you live in provides a human being with so many material goods that it totally, or at least to a great extent, forgets that meaning in life and contentment are intimately interwoven. A big part of your technical skill is concentrated on improving your material needs, while the rest of it is used for destructive purposes. Therefore you sacrifice to this golden calf the whole of your time on earth. You work, you rush around and you strain yourselves, and you think it is necessary to do this in order to earn the money for the material goods you think you need. Your whole system is progressively built up in this way, and the little children who incarnate on your earth become new little consumers. There is a big industry built up around these little consumers, but these little consumers have one big need and that is to be allowed to find their forms in lovable, secure surroundings.
>
> To be contented and to feel meaningfulness are intimately connected, but there is often no meaningfulness in the kind of existence which you have built up. I must also say, for the sake of clarity, that there is nothing wrong with material goods. But the way you chase after them prevents you from feeling the joy of them. As long as you are more concerned with longing and craving for more and more instead of enjoying what you have, you will experience a cause and effect reaction. You see it both in your milieu, in nature and in your homes and cities. The feeling of joy and gratefulness is a very attractive power and will always draw to you what you need. The quicker you understand this process of cause and effect, the greater meaning and happiness it will give you to change your style of living, even if this is ever so difficult.[5]

The next point to consider is the assertion made in an

earlier paragraph that once basic needs are met, happiness does not depend on possessing things, but on attitude to life – human, animal and what is embraced by the word nature. Let us begin with human life, with our attitude to people.

Although it is dangerous to generalise about a subject which is as vast and complex as personal relations, it is none the less possible to make certain observations which have wide application. One such observation is the importance of forgetting self when in the presence of another person. Though initially, and somewhat paradoxically, forgetting self may begin, for example in conversation, as a somewhat self-conscious process, in time and with persistence it will develop into an entirely natural and unselfconscious habit. Attention can then be focussed, wholly and at once, on the other person, unless or until the other person – out of genuine concern, not just as a matter of politeness – focusses his (or her) attention on you. Out of focussed attention which includes feeling as well as thinking – sometimes referred to as empathy – and which is devoid of any undertone of self, there arises almost inevitably a sense of concern, and then of caring, i.e. of love. Happiness can rarely, if ever, be obtained directly. But it often comes when self has been forgotten during the performance of some necessary or worthwhile activity. Conflicting thoughts and feelings have died down, and for the time being there is peace, harmony and happiness. Three centuries ago Sir Isaac Newton discovered three laws of motion, the third of which is normally stated in the form 'Action and reaction are equal and opposite.' Though all three laws were formulated in connection with purely material bodies and particles, I have always suspected that the third law has, in fact, far wider application, cf. 'For what measure ye mete, it shall be measured to you again',[6] and what the Teacher in *The Wheel of Rebirth* has to say:

Nothing is denied you but what you deny yourself. Do you desire friends and lovers, then give friendship and love, and they will crowd around you. Give service and you will be served; heal others and your own diseases will be cured. If anything ever seems to be denied you, give of that thing freely and eventually through giving, you will receive [but not necessarily in the present incarnation]. If the world appears to ill-treat you, look well, my son, into your own heart; you will surely find hidden therein something that is inimical to the world.[7]

Another matter deserving attention is environing conditions. At any given time these may be congenial, or uncongenial, or, what is much more likely, a mixture of the two. What should be our attitude? If something which is uncongenial and causing unhappiness can be changed, there is no problem. If, however, it cannot be changed, what then? Stripped down to bare essentials the problem has three constituents: X, the ostensible cause of the trouble, not necessarily an individual; P, the person experiencing the trouble; and R, the relationship between P and X. As R is unsatisfactory, and X cannot be altered, the only hope of improvement is for P to change. If P's attitude to life has been, and continues to be, one of wants and demands, unhappiness is likely to persist. If, however, P's attitude to life becomes one of observing and learning – learning all that the particular situation has to teach – R, the relationship between P and X, will change. Resentment, for example 'Why should I have to put up with X?', will be replaced by acceptance, acceptance of a situation which may have much to teach and from which much may be learnt. To get thus far is a major step towards the attainment of harmony and peace of mind. This is particularly true of many marriages about which the central character in a book by Cyril Scott points out that 'a trying partner affords a golden opportunity for progress to the soul advanced enough to profit by it'.[8] In all such situations the key word is acceptance. But the acceptance must be positive, i.e. the situation must be entered into fully and with perception. Negative acceptance, devoid of hope or purpose, is an opportunity wasted and worse than useless. The foregoing is very well put by P. G. Bowen in the following cryptic passage from *The Occult Way*.

> When attracted by and involved in any set of Conditions, throw yourself whole-heartedly into the task of experiencing them to the utmost. The results that accrue from this positive activity will take form as negative Powers and will bear you away from the thrall of the Monitors, leaving them but empty shells. Whatever thy hand findeth to do, do it with all thy might.[9]

In relation to happiness, acceptance is important also from another angle. During the Christian era the emphasis in the West has tended to be on doing rather than on being and one of the results of the recent upsurge of interest in Zen has been to emphasise the importance of being. In particular, it has advocated taking the present and whatever the present may comprise, and experiencing it in detail and to the full, as exemplified in *The Zen of Seeing* by Frederick Franck,[10] and in *Zen and the Art of Motor Cycle Maintenance* by Robert M. Pirsig.[11] Such an attitude makes for happiness, because it embodies a deliberate effort to forget self-centred desires and wants, and to enter into a relationship with what is, both human and non human. Such an attitude is very similar to the advice given on p. 161 of Chapter 11 by P. G. Bowen's teacher: 'Let him find his chief happiness in that of others . . . his knowledge in the myriad changes and cycles of nature.'

Regarding our attitude to life, attention has so far been directed to human life. What can be said about our attitude to animal life and to what is embraced by the word nature? Once again, the key word is harmony. Where there is harmony there is happiness; where there is disharmony there is not. Two obvious examples are the shepherd and his dog, and the rider and his horse, when working together as partners in a team. The mutual understanding and harmony so achieved is deeply satisfying to the human member of the team and a delight to the beholder. More generally, if man's attitude to animals and to nature is governed by compassion and understanding, there will be harmony and happiness. But in so far as these two qualities are absent and are replaced by ruthlessness and lack of understanding, the outcome will be unhappy, and may eventually be disastrous. This is shown very clearly by the following allegory.

There were once two kingdoms – the Kingdom of the Present, and the Kingdom of the Future. And the Ruler of the Present had important documents which were due for immediate delivery to the Ruler of the Future. To fulfil this obligation, the Ruler of the Present summoned an envoy, and provided him with a horse appropriate for a long and arduous journey. The envoy was supplied with provisions, and was equipped with crop and spurs. In this allegory, the envoy is humanity, the horse is nature and the documents are the inalienable birthright of children yet unborn. The crop represents methods of increasing animal (re)production; the spurs symbolise chemicals for applying to food and earth and water. If used compassionately and with understanding crop and spurs can serve a right and useful purpose. But if applied ruthlessly and without understanding the horse will be ruined and the envoy will fail to complete his mission. If the mission is to be accomplished successfully there must be complete understanding between the envoy and his horse.

So far we have talked about happiness. What can we say about joy? We have seen that happiness results when the personality is at peace with itself and is in harmony with its surroundings. Joy stems from the attainment of harmony at a deeper level of being – when personality and soul are in alignment. In the writer's experience, working harmoniously with a group of people who are dedicated to something bigger than themselves and are completely loyal to each other is one of the most rewarding things in life and a key to joy. The personal consciousness is subsumed in something noble and greater than itself.

References

1. *Der Cherubinische Wandersmann*, Angelus Silesius, (Insel Verlag, Leipzig)

2. The original German reads: 'Gott gebe mir die Gelassenheit Dinge hinzunehmen, die ich nicht andern kann; den Mut Dinge zu andern, die ich andern kann; und die Weisheit das eine vom anderen zu unterscheiden.' The English translation is due to Reinhold Niebuhr

3. *Meister Eckhart*, translation by Raymond B. Blakney, (Harper & Row, New York, 1941). Talks of Instruction No. 23

4. *Some Sayings of the Buddha*, translated by F. L. Woodward, (Oxford University Press, World's Classics Edition, 1951. First published 1925), p. 8

5. *Let Life Live*, Gita Keiller, (The Mitre Press, 1975), p. 19

6. Luke 6:38

7. *The Wheel of Rebirth*, H. K. Challoner, (Theosophical Publishing House, 1969. First published by Rider & Co., 1935), p. 111

8. *The Initiate in the New World*, Cyril Scott, (George Routledge & Sons, 1932), p. 116

9. *The Occult Way*, P. G. Bowen, (The Occult Book Society, 1938), p. 109

10. *The Zen of Seeing*, Frederick Franck, (Wildwood House, London, 1973)

11. *Zen and the Art of Motor Cycle Maintenance*, Robert M. Pirsig, (The Bodley Head, 1974)

15: Implications for Education

The doomwatchers predict a total collapse of our civilisation, and they have some very convincing evidence to back it up. But I do not believe that collapse is inevitable and I am convinced that the key to survival is in the universities. It is their responsibility to achieve that balance between technology and theology which seems to be so essential to a healthy society. When that happens and when fact and inspiration can walk hand in hand once again, then the intellectual and aesthetic training offered by the universities will result in the advancement of civilisation and the enlightenment and refinement of taste.[1]

Duke of Edinburgh

I believe that there are unmistakable trends that the world of human society is moving towards a great synthesis.
The primary aim of education in the West . . . has been and still is the intellectual development of men . . . to create doctors, scientists, engineers, to go to outer space . . . what is external is very clearly perceived, while . . . what is inside of us remains a dark jungle tract.
In the East . . . the stress is the other way around. *Traditionally* the primary objective of oriental education . . . has been the development of the moral and spiritual qualities of men . . . to try to discover what is inside of us . . . At the same time the intellectual aspect of life has been ignored . . .
My feeling is that a pure intellectual development, unaccompanied by a corresponding moral and spiritual development, is sure to lead humanity from one crisis to another. At the same time, pure moral and spiritual development without a corresponding intellectual development, will be just an anachronism in this second half of the twentieth century. So I think it would be wise for all of us,

212

the peoples from the West as well as the peoples from the East, to try to understand these two basically different concepts and harmonise them so that human development will be fully integrated in all three aspects, intellectual, moral and spiritual . . .[2]

U Thant

During 1968 there was widespread and sometimes serious student unrest in many universities and colleges. In Britain the unrest was unexpected, and its outbreak took most of those in authority by surprise. What was the cause of this phenomenon? What had gone wrong? And when things did go wrong, how could those in authority deal with the situation?

In the university where I was at the time and which, though small, was more or less typical, about three quarters of the students were fairly conventional in their attitude and outlook and were only concerned with their courses, sport and social activities. About a fifth were the thinkers, pioneers, doers and trend setters. The political malcontents, amorally subservient to their iconoclastic ideal, and the psychologically disturbed, projecting onto their environment their own psychological shortcomings, made up the remainder. The procedure adopted by the political malcontents, readily backed by the disturbed minority, was to pick on some matter which they thought could be worked up into a grievance, and then do all in their power to promote a confrontation with the university authorities, and enlist support for their actions from more moderate elements in the student body. In doing this the political malcontents did not feel bound by any ethical considerations. Only two principles received their whole hearted support. These were: (i) that the present organisation of society is so rotten that it is beyond hope of redemption and must be totally destroyed; (ii) that the end justified the means, and that it is therefore not incumbent to tell the truth unless it is in the interests of (i) to do so. If it were possible in a relaxed moment (not always easy of achievement) to put

213

the question: 'When you have been successful in destroying the present organisation of society, with what will you replace it?' The answer was: 'Vested interests are so powerful that destruction will take time. When we're well on our way to achieving that, we'll consider what to set up instead.' Protests by 2 or 3 per cent of the student body should be capable of containment. But if the percentage exceeded 10, as it sometimes did, the situation became more difficult, and meant that a significant number of moderate students had thrown in their lot with the militants. Why? This seemed to me then, and seems to me now, the most significant aspect of the troubles of twenty years ago.

If it is agreed, as suggested in the Personal Introduction, that 'an age of authority is passing away and with it are disappearing many cherished beliefs and practices', then surely this yields a clue to what is missing, to wit, a generally acceptable framework for living, a meaningful philosophy of life. In the words of the Teacher referred to in Chapters 7 and 8, 'There will be political difficulties amongst the young. The reason for this is the failure of their teachers and elders; nothing constructive leading to the full flowering of the personality has been shown them. They have merely been taught with cynicism that everything that is established at the moment is by that fact wrong, *but nothing durable, lasting, noble has been put in its place.*' For a minority of students – and not just students – religious belief, as normally understood and taught, provides the looked-for guidelines. But for the majority – as a statement of fact – it does not, and there has developed a vacuum, ready to be filled with cults and ideologies, of which many are questionable, and some are undesirable or worse. In varying measure, many students are aware of this need, and some are looking in strange places to meet it. With lessening authority and the accompanying relaxation of constraint, has come an increase in freedom – freedom to speak, write and act, in ways which a generation ago would not have been tolerated. But predictably, though contrary to the expectation of many, this increase in freedom has not led to a corresponding increase in happiness. A life which is free from all restraint (in so far as that is practicable) is psychologically exhausting because it is intensely boring. This may be hard to believe without the practical experience, yet in the 1930s, there was in the South of France a community of English-speaking people who lived lives which were permissive to a high degree. They were wealthy people who had nothing to do but amuse themselves. Yet the suicide rate was amongst the highest in the world. Why? Because after a time a life of permissiveness *which lacks any synthesising principle* provides little or no satisfaction. Psychologically it just does not work. It is the exact opposite of what is described in the prayer book by that beautiful and penetrating phrase 'in whose service is perfect freedom'.

Before the Second World War, the choice of a career, what to do after graduation, played a prominent part in most students' thinking. Today priorities are different. How to achieve satisfactory personal relationships has become top priority in the minds of many students. The choice of a career, and career prospects, have dropped to second place. Though the current level of unemployment, and of graduate unemployment in particular, has tended both to modify this change of outlook and to inhibit outbreaks of student unrest, a fundamental shift of attitude remains a fact. And with it has come the realisation that satisfactory relationships depend on the parties concerned being honest with themselves and with each other. Students today want to try to think and act for themselves, and are not so willing to do what they think others expect of them. While realising that they are part of society, they do not feel bound as formerly by the usually accepted social conventions. Several years ago, in some newspaper or journal, the writer was struck by a cartoon. It showed three men in a pub. Two of the men, who were talking to each other in low tones, appeared puzzled and worried. They were casting uneasy glances over their shoulders at the third man, who looked relaxed and at ease conversing with the barman at the end of the counter. Of the two men whispering together, said one to the other: 'I don't understand how he gets away with it, he is just himself.' Today's students would get the point at once. When I read in the press that some senior politician has spent the vacation 'improving his/her image', I shudder.

Compared to the pre-war years, students are much more widely, though perhaps more superficially, informed, and on average more sophisticated. The mass media have seen to that; and, of course, travel. Before the Second World War it was comparatively unusual for students to travel abroad; today the reverse is true. Students as a whole are no less idealistic than in the past, and are particularly incensed by what they deem to be unjust or hypocritical. But they are more realistic, and are more perspicacious about what constitutes injustice or hypocrisy. A realisation of this fact is vital to an understanding of student attitudes, and within a university or college underlines the importance of locating and dealing with possible causes of trouble before it actually erupts. And the importance of *never covering up*. That last is crucial, for if trouble does break out, it will take the form of a battle for the hearts and minds of uncommitted middle of the road students. On one side are the militants who have picked on something which it has been possible to present as a grievance. On the other side are the Vice-Chancellor or Principal and his administrators. The militants will stick at nothing in their efforts to exploit the situation since, for them, distortion of the facts, including downright fabrication, is entirely justified by the end in view. And if the situation becomes difficult, there can always be an appeal to 'student solidarity'. The role of the administration is simple – in theory if not in practice! It can be summed up in the one word 'candour'. The Vice-Chancellor or Principal must be completely candid about the facts relating to the original grievance and any subsequent developments and, no matter how great the provocation, he must stick to his own rules.

For the writer these were 'never make a rule which you can't enforce, never make a promise which you can't keep and never make a threat which you can't carry out'. The most important word in these three rules is NEVER, which brooks of no exception whatever. For 95 per cent of the time, it is really very easy; but for 5 per cent of the time it may be very hard. And that is when it matters. One of the more heart-warming experiences which came the way of the writer was to receive a letter out of the blue from an erstwhile militant student saying: 'You taught me the importance of honesty at both a public and private level. It took me a while to learn the lesson but, on reflection, I can see that it is the only way to work.' As the conflict proceeds and in an endeavour to maintain their support, the militants' statements and accusations are liable to become more extreme. When this happens, and provided the administration has done nothing to justify the accusations, the credibility of the militants will be called in question by the middle of the road students and support for the disruption will start to crumble. During the period of disruption the militants will issue a steady stream of literature. It is essential that the administration does the same, answering point by point and without exaggeration the statements and accusations made by the militants. Negotiations will certainly be frequent and will often be prolonged.

About the world scene many students are far from happy. For example they ask what is being done by the rich nations to help the poor nations. Though the provision of economic aid is certainly not the complete answer, it is a factor. But when account is taken of what the developing countries are paying in interest on money already borrowed, the financial help which most of the developing countries are receiving is pitifully small. When the rich countries maintain that they are giving all they can afford, many students regard such an attitude as completely hypocritical. This country's contribution is well short of the UN target for official development assistance of 0.7 per cent of the gross national product.

Or take the industrial-military complex in various countries. The scale of it is illustrated by the fact that 'What the world spends in one day on arms would support the work of UNICEF (United Nations International Childrens Emergency Fund) for ten years. A number of other comparisons are given in Chapter 2 of *The War Games that Superpowers Play*, published by The London Centre for International Peacebuilding.[3] Having regard to the increasingly destructive power of nuclear weapons, the almost complete absence of an alternative approach, *pursued with vigour and imagination*, is viewed by many with apprehension verging on despair.

And what about education? The Government's aim that everyone should be both literate and numerate, and that as many members of the community as possible should acquire some manual skill, and should be able to write clearly, speak clearly and think clearly about any matter that comes up for consideration, is wholly good. But it is only half the picture. The question arises – education for what?

Today, as a result of automation and computers, there are clear indications that in future the goods which people need can be produced in a technologically developed country by fewer and fewer persons. In a socially responsible society this means that essential work will be shared, and that many people will have more free time, perhaps much more if significant disarmament comes about. But increase in leisure time will not bring satisaction unless people are educated to face and accept the opportunity and challenge that goes with it, that is, to understand and appreciate the other half of the picture – that life is for living, and what this implies.

These, and many similar examples, indicate that today the overriding need for the young, and the not so young too, is the provision of a satisfying purpose; something which will serve to coordinate and synthesise the forces in our society. What then is to be done? Change the educational system? No! Changing the system would, of itself, achieve little or nothing. The need is for a change in attitude of mind – by many parents and many teachers. What is required is the realisation that every young person has an inalienable right to have put before him or her some star, some source of inspiration, some guiding light. So much of the emphasis today is on raising the material standard of living, fostered in certain quarters with an injection of nationalistic fervour. But this will not satisfy indefinitely.[4] It is not that there is anything wrong with raising the material standard of living. Indeed, for more than half the world it is essential.[5] But that is not the point. What is wrong is the failure of the rich countries in the Western World to realise that 'man does not live by bread alone', and that what ought to be a means has become the goal. The material standard of living has become an end in itself[6] and, in the process, as Sir Kelvin points out in his Foreword, 'Mankind seems to have lost all sense of purpose.'

At a Conference on New Themes for Education held at Dartington Hall in April 1976, the educational psychologist James Hemming said:

> It is now plain that education in general, and secondary and tertiary education in particular, are hopelessly biased towards the objective, logical, intellectual side. Education of the subjective, intuitional and aesthetic aspects of personality, in contrast, is, for the most part, desperately thin. This might be called the missing factor in education, which results in lop-sided curricula, low motivation, and distorted personality development.

Expressed in physiological terms current education is primarily concerned with developing the left hemisphere of the cerebral cortex – the part equipped to handle experience and response which is linear, logical and rational – and much less concerned with developing the right hemisphere – the part concerned with what is non-linear, holistic and intuitive.[7] In the experience of the writer many students are keenly aware of, and deeply disturbed by, this lack of balance. Many more are aware that something is wrong, but

219

are not able to define what it is. That education should have developed in this way is not surprising when it is realised that what is 'linear, logical and rational' can be measured and assessed; whereas what is 'non-linear, holistic and intuitive' is both more difficult to assess and more difficult to teach. But the need to rectify this unbalance is vital.

What is becoming increasingly clear is that the need for a fresh synthesis, a new metaphysic which is supported by experiment and experience, is urgent. For so much of the emphasis today is on means. Ends, questions relating to the meaning and purpose of life, are referred to but rarely. A welcome exception is *A Guide for the Perplexed* by E. F. Schumacher.[8] So long as this unbalance continues, trouble, in one form or another, will never be very far away. Moreover, so much of what is taught in schools, colleges and universities is expounded as a purely intellectual exercise by people who often have little belief in, or are even in sympathy with, what they are saying.[9] In the words of the Teacher quoted on p. 105, Chapter 7, 'So much that is written is written from the intellect. The words are dead words, uninspired, and fail to draw forth from the reader that raising of the consciousness into another realm that flows from the union of soul and personality.'

But there is no need for the outlook to be so uninspiring and the ground to look so parched. This book provides plenty of evidence to show that Hamlet was right when he said 'There are more things in heaven and earth, Horatio, than are dreamt of in your philosophy.'[10] Although the five propositions listed below have certainly not been proved, there is at least a significant and growing body of evidence to warrant their thorough examination and to merit reflection on their implications.

(1)   That man, when alive, can function as a self-conscious being independently of his physical body.

(2)   That man's consciousness survives the death of his physical body.

(3)   That the etheric body and the chakras have objective existence in our three-dimensional space-time world.

(4)   That reincarnation embodies a profound truth.

(5)   That the soul (as referred to in this book) is a reality.

And if, as this book suggests, the purpose of the school of life on this planet is 'to educate its pupils to perform on the stage of life whatever parts they are called upon to play with grace, skill and selfless dedication', there is no lack of material with which to construct a significantly different background for a lot of current education. Among other things it would lead to a realisation that we are in very truth all members of one family, and that until the attainment of spiritual maturity so we shall remain. 'Them' and 'us' might come to be regarded in a rather different light when it is realised that in another incarnation the roles might be reversed. And a similar change might occur regarding the urgency of our attitude to the four freedoms enunciated by President Roosevelt in January 1941:

Freedom of speech and expression – everywhere in the world. Freedom of every person to worship God in his own way – everywhere in the world. Freedom from want – which, translated into world terms, means economic understanding which will secure to every nation a healthy peacetime life for its inhabitants – everywhere in the world. Freedom from fear – which, translated into world terms, means a worldwide reduction of armaments to such a point and in such a thorough fashion that no nation will be in a position to commit an act of physical aggression against any neighbour – anywhere in the world.

What is strange, and greatly to be regretted, is that so little effort is being put into investigating the five propositions listed above by those who are qualified to do so. Although it has long been the tradition in Britain to give to the individual researcher the maximum possible freedom, since no one can know for certain what a particular line of research will lead to, it is surely only common sense to *encourage* lines of research which, if successful, are likely to be *either* practically useful *or* metaphysically significant (i.e. shed light on the meaning and purpose of life). Though the five propositions are unquestionably of very great metaphysical significance, the number of departments in British universities and polytechnics which are actively working in such fields is still very very small. Something of an exception has been the formation during the early 1970s of 'The Scientific and Medical Network',[11] an informal and growing group of qualified scientists and doctors, now numbering over four hundred, who 'seek to extend the framework of contemporary thought beyond the ideas at present considered orthodox and to create a situation in which science can adopt a much more comprehensive approach to human problems, taking into account the relevance of intuitive and spiritual insights'.

In conclusion, two quotations:

> The task of all true educators is to bring light to the minds of those they instruct so that they may walk more securely in the way which leads to the goal for any particular incarnation.[12]

> The entire trend of the present urge forward is to enable the race to acquire knowledge, to transmute it into wisdom by the aid of the understanding, and thus to become 'fully enlightened'. *Enlightenment is the major goal of education.*[13]

References

1. From an address given by the Duke of Edinburgh at Adelaide University in 1974. A shortened version was published in *Frontier* titled 'Universities and the Diffusion of Culture'
2. Remarks made by U Thant, when Secretary General of the United Nations, to a Non-Governmental Organisation Conference
3. *The War Games that Superpowers Play*, D. M. A. Leggett & C. M. Waterlow, (The London Centre for International Peacebuilding, 3rd ed., 1985)

IMPLICATIONS FOR EDUCATION

4. 'A World Divided', Alexander Solzenitsyn. Address given at the 1978 Harvard Commencement Ceremony
5. See *The Sane Alternative*, James Robertson, (Villiers Publications, London, 1978)
6. See *Small is Beautiful*, E. F. Schumacher, (Blond & Briggs, 1973)
7. *The Nature of Human Consciousness*, Robert E. Ornstein, (W. H. Freeman & Co., San Francisco, 1973)
8. *A Guide for the Perplexed*, E. F. Schumacher, (Jonathan Cape, 1977)
9. *A Kind of Belief*, Michael Duke and Eric Whitton, (Published for the General Synod Board of Education by the Church Information Office, 1977)
10. *Hamlet*, Shakespeare, Act I, Scene 5
11. Until November 1986, Hon. Sec. was G. B. Blaker. Since then it is David Lorimer, The Old School House, Hampnett, Northleach, Glos.
12. *Discipleship in the New Age*, Alice A. Bailey, (Lucis Publishing Co., New York, 1944), Vol. 1, p. 177
13. *Education in the New Age*, Alice A. Bailey, (Lucis Press, 1954), p. 52

223

Epilogue

From *The Idyll of the White Lotus*[1]

The young priest rose and stood beside me, while I still gazed upon the glory.

'Hear me, my brother,' he said. 'There are three truths which are absolute, and which cannot be lost, but yet may remain silent for lack of speech.

'The soul of man is immortal, and its future is the future of a thing whose growth and splendour has no limit.

'The principle which gives life dwells in us and without us, is undying and eternally beneficent, is not heard or seen, or smelt, but is perceived by the man who desires perception.

'Each man is his own absolute lawgiver, the dispenser of glory or gloom to himself; the decreer of his life, his reward, his punishment.

'These truths, which are as great as is life itself, are as simple as the simplest mind of man. Feed the hungry with them. Farewell. It is sundown. They will come for thee; be thou ready.'

He was gone. But the glory did not fade from before my eyes. I saw the truth. I saw the light.

From a Hindu Scripture[2]

The Great Singer built the worlds, and the universe is His song.

References

1. *The Idyll of the White Lotus*, Mabel Collins, (The Theosophical Publishing House, Adyar, Madras, 1884), p. 123
2. *A Treatise on White Magic*, Alice A. Bailey, (Lucis Publishing Company, 5th edition, 1951. First published 1934), p. 142

Appendix I

One of the most beautiful examples of the scientific method is the discovery of Neptune in the middle of the last century.

Observational astronomers had noticed that Uranus was not behaving in a normal manner. By a very small amount it was deviating from its orbit. Why? This was the problem to be solved. An accurate description of the deviations constituted Stage 1, collecting the relevant data. Stage 2, framing a hypothesis, consisted of Adams and Leverrier postulating the existence of another planet as the cause of the deviations, and predicting where such a planet would be – if it existed. Stage 3, checking the hypothesis, was performed by Galle looking through his telescope at the spot calculated by Adams and Leverrier and seeing, for the first time, the planet which was subsequently called Neptune.

Now let us examine the three stages of the scientific method so as to see the kind of reasoning process required at each stage.

About Stage 1, collecting the relevant data, there is little to be said except to emphasise the importance of judgement in relation to what is, or is not, relevant. To illustrate the kind of judgement required, suppose that a comet had been spotted before Uranus was observed to be perturbed from its orbit. Would this have been relevant data? If the two events, the presence of the comet and the perturbation of Uranus, had taken place at the same time, quite possibly. But, as we are supposing that one event preceded the other by an adequate interval of time, it is, on the face of it, most unlikely that the two are connected. Any data collected about, say, the comet's path would therefore be irrelevant.

And so to Stage 2, framing a hypothesis. This is an example of inductive reasoning, of arguing from the particular to the general; of arguing from the particular behaviour of Uranus over a short period of time to the general existence of another planet. A hypothesis, which, if true, would explain and predict a great deal more than the observations which prompted the investigation in the first place. In the case of a scientific genius, however, this inductive reasoning stage may cease to be reasoning as that word is normally understood, and be instead an example of intuition, that is, of immediate apprehension. The scientific genius may perceive in a flash the single hypothesis which will coordinate a whole range of previously uncorrelated phenomena.

Finally, Stage 3, checking the hypothesis by suitable experiments or observations. This was looking through the telescope to see if there was anything near where Adams and Leverrier had predicted. While not forgetting the part played by imagination, this stage is essentially an example of arguing from the general to the particular, that is, of deductive reasoning.

Appendix II

'These are the Ten Commandments that, as a teacher, I should wish to promulgate' wrote Bertrand Russell in 1951 when asked to define the essence of the liberal attitude.

1. Do not feel absolutely certain of anything.
2. Do not think it worth while to proceed by concealing evidence, for the evidence is sure to come to light.
3. Never try to discourage thinking for you are sure to succeed.
4. When you meet with opposition, even if it should be from your husband or your children, endeavour to overcome it by argument and not by authority, for a victory dependent upon authority is unreal and illusory.
5. Have no respect for the authority of others, for there are always contrary authorities to be found.
6. Do not use power to suppress opinions you think pernicious, for if you do the opinions will suppress you.
7. Do not fear to be eccentric in opinion, for every opinion now accepted was once eccentric.
8. Find more pleasure in intelligent dissent than in passive agreement, for, if you value intelligence as you should, the former implies a deeper agreement than the latter.
9. Be scrupulously truthful, even if the truth is inconvenient, for it is more inconvenient when you try to conceal it.
10. Do not feel envious of the happiness of those who live in a fool's paradise, for only a fool will think that it is happiness.

Bibliography

The number of books relating to the subject matter of *The Sacred Quest* is very great. The books listed below are those which the writer has read or consulted and has found helpful. Some are referred to in the text and are included in the references at the end of the relevant chapter. Putting the titles under headings, though inevitably somewhat arbitrary, seemed preferable to a lengthy alphabetical list with no indication of subject matter except the title. Dates usually refer to first published, or first published in English if publication is initially in some other language.

General Background

C. D. Broad, *Religion, Philosophy and Psychical Research*, Routledge & Kegan Paul, 1953

J. Bronowski, *The Ascent of Man*, B.B.C. Publications, 1973

Alexis Carrel, *Man, the Unknown*, Hamish Hamilton, 1935

Kenneth Clarke, *Civilisation*, B.B.C. Publications, 1969

Ronald Higgins, *The Seventh Enemy*, Hodder & Stoughton, 1978

William James, *The Varieties of Religious Experience – a study in human nature*, Gifford Lectures, 1901–02. Longmans, Green, 1952

Raynor C. Johnson, *The Imprisoned Splendour*, Hodder & Stoughton, 1953

W. Macneile Dixon, *The Human Situation*, Gifford Lectures, 1935–37. Arnold, 1946. First published, 1937

E. F. Schumacher, *Small is Beautiful – a study of economics as if people mattered*, Blond & Briggs, 1973

BIBLIOGRAPHY

Pierre Teilhard de Chardin, *The Phenomenon of Man*, Collins, 1959

Philosophy

John Hick, *Death and Eternal Life*, Collins, 1976
Hywel D. Lewis, *The Self and Immortality*, Macmillan, 1973

Religion, Religious Experience, Mysticism

Fritjof Capra, *The Tao of Physics – an exploration of the parallels between modern physics and eastern mysticism*, Wildwood House, 1975
Donald Coggan, *The Heart of the Christian Faith*, Collins, 1978
F. C. Happold, *Religious Faith and Twentieth Century Man*, Penguin Books, 1960
Alister Hardy, *The Spiritual Nature of Man: a study of contemporary religious experience*, O.U.P., 1980
Richard Harries, *Being a Christian*, Mowbray, 1981
Martin Israel, *Summons to Life*, Hodder & Stoughton, 1974
Martin Israel, *Precarious Living*, Hodder & Stoughton, 1976
Raynor C. Johnson, *A Religious Outlook for Modern Man*, Hodder & Stoughton, 1963
Keith Ward, *The Living God*, S.P.C.K., 1984
C. S. Lewis, *Mere Christianity*, Geoffrey Bles, 1952
P. D. Mehta, *Early Indian Religious Thought – an introduction and essay*, Luzac, 1956
S. Radhakrishnan, *Eastern Religions and Western Thought*, O.U.P., 1939
Peter Spink, *Spiritual Man in a New Age*, Darton, Longman & Todd, 1980
Wellesley Tudor Pole and Rosamond Lehmann, *A Man Seen Afar*, Neville Spearman, 1965
Stephen Verney, *Into the New Age*, Fontana, 1976
Leslie D. Weatherhead, *The Christian Agnostic*, Hodder & Stoughton, 1965

229

Extra Sensory Perception

Frances Banks, *Frontiers of Revelation*, Max Parrish, 1962
Robert Crookall, *The Study and Practice of Astral Projection*, Aquarian Press, 1961
Rosalind Heywood, *The Sixth Sense – an enquiry into extrasensory perception*, Chatto & Windus, 1959
Rosalind Heywood, *The Infinite Hive – a personal record of extrasensory experiences*, Chatto & Windus, 1964
Shafica Karagulla, *Breakthrough to Creativity – your higher sense perception*, De Vorse, Santa Monica, California, 1967
Lawrence LeShan, *The Medium, the Mystic, and the Physicist – toward a general theory of the paranormal*, Turnstone Press, 1974
Lyall Watson, *Supernature – the natural history of the supernatural*, Hodder & Stoughton, 1973
Robert A. Monroe, *Journeys out of the Body*, Doubleday, New York, 1971
Phoebe Payne, *Man's Latent Powers*, Faber & Faber, 1938
P. D. Payne and L. J. Bendit, *The Psychic Sense*, Faber & Faber, 1943

Near Death Experiences

Margot Grey, *Return from Death*, Arkana, 1985
Maurice Rawlings, *Beyond Death's Door*, Sheldon Press, 1979
K. Ring, *Life at Death*, Coward, McCann & Geoghegan, New York, 1980
George Ritchie and Elizabeth Sherrill, *Return from Tomorrow*, Kingsway Publications, 1978

Survival

Paul Beard, *Survival of Death*, Psychic Press, 1966
Paul Beard, *Living On*, George Allen & Unwin, 1980
Robert Crookall, *The Supreme Adventure – analyses of psychic communications*, Published for The Churches' Fellowship for Psychical Study by James Clarke, 1961

Geraldine Cummins, *Swan on a Black Sea*, Routledge & Kegan Paul, 1965

Doris Collins, *A Woman of Spirit*, Granada, 1983

Helen Greaves, *Testimony of Light*, Published for The Churches' Fellowship for Psychical & Spiritual Studies by The World Fellowship Press, 1969

Helen Greaves, *The Wheel of Eternity*, Neville Spearman, 1974

David Lorimer, *Survival? – body, mind and death in the light of psychic experience*, Routledge & Kegan Paul, 1984

Jane Sherwood, *The Country Beyond*, Neville Spearman, 1969

Roger Whitby, *Gateway*, Psychic Press, 1980

Reincarnation

Gina Cerminara, *Many Mansions*, Neville Spearman, 1967

H. K. Challoner, *The Wheel of Rebirth*, Rider, 1935. Theosophical Publishing House, 1969

Joan Grant and Denys Kelsey, *Many Lifetimes*, Gollancz, 1969. Corgi, 1976

Arthur Guirdham, *The Cathars and Reincarnation*, Neville Spearman, 1970

Arthur Guirdham, *We are One Another – a record of group reincarnation*, Neville Spearman, 1974

D. M. A. Leggett and M. G. Payne, *A Forgotten Truth*, Pilgrims Book Services, 1986

Edward Ryall, *Second Time Round*, Neville Spearman, 1974

Ralph Shirley, *The Problem of Rebirth – an enquiry into the basis of the reincarnation hypothesis*, Rider, 1936

Ian Stevenson, *Twenty Cases Suggestive of Reincarnation*, American Society for Psychical Research, 1966

Helen Wambach, *Life before Life*, Bantum Books, 1979

Leslie D. Weatherhead, *The Case for Reincarnation*, (A booklet). M. C. Peto, Tadworth, Surrey, 1958

The Future of Man

Sri Aurobindo, *The Future Evolution of Man*, George Allen & Unwin, 1962

Alice A. Bailey, *A Treatise on White Magic or The Way of the Disciple*, Lucis Press, 5th ed., 1951. First published, 1934

P. G. Bowen, *The Occult Way*, The Occult Book Society, 1938. The Theosophical Publishing House, 1978

P. G. Bowen, *Sayings of the Ancient One*, Rider, 1936. The Theosophical Publishing House, 1986

E. L. Gardner, *The Wider View – studies in The Secret Doctrine*, Theosophical Publishing House, Adyar, Madras, 1962

Aldous Huxley, *The Perennial Philosophy*, Chatto & Windus, 1946

Raynor C. Johnson, *Nurslings of Immortality*, Hodder & Stoughton, 1957

Gita Keiller, *Let Life Live*, Mitre Press, 1975

P. D. Mehta, *The Heart of Religion*, Compton Russell, 1975

Pierre Teilhard de Chardin, *The Future of Man*, Collins, 1964

Kenneth Walker, *So Great a Mystery*, Victor Gollancz, 1958

Index

The Index does not include names which *only* occur explicitly in the Bibliography or in the end of chapter References.

Adams 225
Ajna centre 153, 155, 169
antahkarana 153, 155, 163, 169
Arjuna 170
Arnold, Matthew 43
Ashby, Eric 11
Assagioli, Roberto 146–148
Atlantis, legend of 85
atman 112, 128, 145
authority 3, 32, 128, 213

Bacon, Francis 10
Bailey, Alice A. 61, 122, 128, 136
Balfour, A. J. 189
Banks, Frances 150
Beard, Paul 65, 70
beauty 16, 34, 38, 39, 141, 183
Bede, the Venerable 14
Bendit, Mrs (née Phoebe Payne) 127, 151, 152
Berlin 10
Bhagavad Gita 169, 170, 182
Blake, Maurice 77
Blake, William 44
Blavatsky, H. P. 161
Bolic, A. M. 85
Bologna 9
Boswell, Tyso 77
Bowen, P. G. 74, Chap. 11, 179–182, 189, 209
Boyle 10
Broad, C. D. 1, 65

Brother Mandus 34
Browne, Hugh Junor 65
Browning, Robert 19, 43, 44, 107
Brunton, Paul 55
Buchan, John 45
Buddha 32, 62, 136, 137, 138, 162, 163, 204, 205
Buddhism 1, 83, 108

Cambridge 11
Cathars 80
Cayce, Edgar 76, 77, 109
Cerminara, Gina 77, 109
chakra 152, 155, 169, 221
Challoner, H. K. 74, 76, 110, 122
chemistry 3, 18
Charlottenburg 11
Christ 32, 108, 113, 124–130, 135–140, 143, 144, 154, 162, 163
Christianity 1, 71, 83, 108, 113, 154
Churchill, Winston 24
Cole, Mr 53
Collins, Doris 70
Coombe Tennant, Mrs 64
Costello, Dr 53
Cranston, S. L. 81
Crookall, Robert 68, 69
cults 129, 214
culture 2, 8, 11, 36
Cummins, Geraldine 64
cynicism 14, 214

Darwin, Charles 10
Delphi 123, 144
desire 119, 147, 154, 164, 179, 180, 205, 207
Devi, Lugdi 73
Devi, Shanti 73
Dixon, W. Macneile 19, 24, 42, 51, 71, 194
Djwhal Khul 103, 128, 159, 166
dogma 8, 26, 32
Duke of Edinburgh 26, 27, 212

Eastcott, Michal J. 170
Eckhart, Meister 144, 204
ecstasy 34, 35, 45, 147
Eddington, Arthur 18
education, Chap. 1, 99, 100, Chap. 15
Einstein, Albert 7, 19
Elijah (Elias) 83
Eliot, T. S. 45, 46
Emmaus 68
emotion 31, 113–118, 145, 181, 195
energy 140, 147, 152, 199
energy patterns 121
Erasmus 93
Eutychius 84
evidence 20, 63, 70, 76, 114, 122, 145
evil 105, 171, 187, 190–194
experiment 17, 20, 56, 129, 161

Fausset, H. L'A. 149
fear 22, 24, 39, 62, 102, 161, 168, 171, 176, 195, 196, 200
Fletcher, John 79
Fluck, Rev. P. 78
Franck, Frederick 209
Frank, Anne, diary of 196
freedom 24, 100, 101, 172, 214, 221
freewill 99–101, 172, 192, 201
Freud, S. 148

Frost, Robert 48, 49

Galileo 25, 120
Galle 225
Gerontius, Dream of 177
goodness 176, 177
Gooneratne, Chandra D. S. 1
Göttingen 10
Goya 75
grace 101, 145, 196, 221
Grant, Joan 77
Greaves, Helen 70
Grey, Margot 39
guilt 168
Guirdham, Arthur 80

Hall, Winslow 34
Hamlet 19, 220
Hammarskjöld, Dag 62
happiness 23, 98, 107, 129, 161, 167, 204–207, 209, 210
Happold, F. C. 170
Hardy, Alister C. viii
harmlessness 182, 183
Harvey 10
Head, Joseph 81
Hearin, Edward 78
Hemming, James 7, 219
Hepworth, Rev. Dr 55
Heraclitus 194
Herbart 148
Hercules 165
Hinduism 1, 83, 108, 112, 128
Hodson, Geoffrey 85
Hofmans, Miss 122, 123
hope 22, 98, 208
Hume 71
Huxley, Julian viii
hypnosis 76, 77

illumination 34, 147, 179
imagination 20, 42, 122, 147, 151, 179

intellect 31, 105, 164, 195, 212, 219, 220
intuition 20, 21, 93, 105, 106, 147, 160, 169, 170, 179, 201, 219, 220, 226

Jacobi, Jolande 194
Jesus 32, 62, 83, 106, 113, 124–129, 133, 140, 163, 172, 197
Joan of Arc 51
John the Baptist 83, 125, 128
Johnson, Raynor 33
Johnston, Charles 125, 163
joy 36, 204, 206, 210
judgment, day of 69, 70, 96
Jung, C. G. xi, 31, 62, 144, 148, 159, 171, 194
justice 34, 81, 82, 96, 184, 196, 204
Justinian, Emperor 84

Kabir 144
Kahunas 148
Kant 148
karma 82, 108–111, 168, 184
Keiller, Gita 133, 201, 206
Kekule 21, 22
Kelsey, Denys 77
King, Martin Luther 160
Kingsford, Anna 193
Krishna 169, 170, 181
Krishnamurti 178

Languedoc 80
Lehmann, Rosamond 128
Le Plongeon 85
Leverrier 225
Lorimer, David 70
Lysaght, S. R. 46

Macbeth 22
Magdalene, Mary 129
Masefield, John 47, 48
Massachusetts Institute of Technology 11

matter 15, 94, 95, 114–118, 125, 145, 150, 193
Medawar, Peter 21
metaphysic 23, 26, 222
monad 128, 145
Monroe, Robert A. 56
Moody, Raymond 58
Myers, Frederick 46
mysticism Chap. 4, 114

NDE (near death experience) 37–39
Newman, Cardinal 10
Newton, Isaac 10, 18, 19
Nicodemus 163

Oetinger, Christoph 204
Origen 83, 84
OOB (out-of-body experience) 51–61
Oxenham, John 178
Oxford 9, 11

Palestine 124, 143
paranormal 1, 17, Chap. 5, 108, 114, 118, 119
Paris 9
Patanjali, Aphorisms of 71, 93, 98, 113, 114, 119, 125
Payne, Phoebe – see Bendit
Penington, Isaac 189
philosophy 2, 71
philosophy of life 4, 8, 11, 214
physics 3, 18
Pirsig, Robert 209
Plato 7, 71, 85
Plotinus 33, 71
Polynesia 148
Poseidonis 85
prana 152
precognition 17, 51, 81
pride 181, 191
probability 63

progress 96, 98–100, 106, 107, 140, 164, 197
proof 16, 96, 122, 162
purpose 11, 19, 101, 105, 106, 200
purpose of life 1, 12, 22, 26, Chaps 7–9, 145, 196, 218–222
psychical research 1, 2
psychology 18, 146, 171
psychosynthesis 146–148
Pythagoras 23, 71

Ralphs, Lincoln 7
Ramsey, Ian 10
redemption 159
reincarnation 47, 51, 70–86, 107–111, 221
religion 25, 26, 31–33, 113, 126–130, 136, 140–143, 181
repentance 168, 190, 191
Roosevelt, President 221
Rossetti, Dante Gabriel 48
Russell, Bertrand 14, 22, 227
Russell, George (A.E.) 42, 74, 93, 106, 135
Ruysbroeck 33
Ryall, E. W. 76, 79

Saint Augustine 113
Saint Paul 55, 187
Salerno 11
Samona, Alexandrina 71, 72
Schoneberg Setzer, J. 11
Schopenhauer 71
Schumacher, E. F. 220
science 2, 3, 10–12, 16–22, 101, 161, 222
scientific method 17–20, 225, 226
Scott, Cyril 208
Shakespeare 107
Shelley 42
Sherwood, Jane 70
Shirley, Ralph 71
Silesius, Angelus 204

sin 190, 191
skill 7, 101, 102, 104, 111, 145, 165, 196, 218, 221
Socrates 51
Spencer, Kelvin vii–x, 219
Sprigg, George 65
Sri Ram, N. 15
Stephens, James 193
Stevenson, Ian 73–76, 79
suffering 166, 185, 189, 192, 193, 195–202, 204, 205
survival 26, 62–70, 121, 122
synthesis 9, 11, 12, 212, 215, 220

telepathy 51, 63, 66, 122, 123
Theodora 84
theology 9, 212
Thompson, Francis 49
Toyne, Clarice 122
Trevelyan, G. M. 2
truth 19, 34, 51, 100, 106, 113, 117, 133, 138, 161, 176, 182–184, 213, 221
Tudor Pole, Wellesley 59, 127, 128

Underhill, Evelyn 32, 36
universities 8–11, 212–217
U Thant 24, 25, 212, 213

values 14
van der Leeuw, J. J. 192
vanity 65, 176, 181
Velikovsky, I. 86
vice 175–177
Vigilius, Pope 84
virtue 117, 175–177, 182–185, 191

Wambach, Helen 77
Weatherhead, Leslie 35, 67, 166
Weisz-Roos, Mrs 75
Wells, H. G. vii

INDEX

Wheeler, Mr 52
will 25, 36, 110, 118, 126, 135, 139, 162, 168, 179, 204
Willett, Mrs 64
wisdom 7, 8, 106, 115, 123, 129,

159, 161, 164, 171, 176, 179, 222
Wordsworth x, 50

Zürich 11

Note
The following words occur so frequently throughout the text that it was considered pointless to include them in the index:
consciousness, death, experience, God, knowledge, law, love, personality, soul, spirit.